Regression Analysis

Regression Analysis

Understanding and Building Business and Economic Models Using Excel

Second Edition

J. Holton Wilson, Barry P. Keating,
and Mary Beal

BEP BUSINESS EXPERT PRESS

Regression Analysis: Understanding and Building Business and Economic Models Using Excel, Second Edition

First published in 2012 by
Business Expert Press, LLC
222 East 46th Street, New York, NY 10017
www.businessexpertpress.com

ISBN-13: 978-1-63157-385-9 (paperback)
ISBN-13: 978-1-63157-386-6 (e-book)

Business Expert Press Quantitative Approaches to Decision Making Collection

Collection ISSN: 2163-9515 (print)
Collection ISSN: 2163-9582 (electronic)

Cover and interior design by Exeter Premedia Services Private Ltd., Chennai, India

First edition: 2012
Second edition: 2016

10 9 8 7 6 5 4 3 2 1

Printed in the United States of America.

Abstract

This book covers essential elements of building and understanding regression models in a business/economic context in an intuitive manner. The technique of regression analysis is used so often in business and economics today that an understanding of its use is necessary for almost everyone engaged in the field. It is especially useful for those engaged in working with numbers—preparing forecasts, budgeting, estimating the effects of business decisions, and any of the forms of analytics that have recently become so useful.

This book is a nontheoretical treatment that is accessible to readers with even a limited statistical background. This book specifically does not cover the theory of regression; it is designed to teach the correct use of regression, while advising the reader of its limitations and teaching about common pitfalls. It is useful for business professionals, MBA students, and others with a desire to understand regression analysis without having to work through tedious mathematical/statistical theory.

This book describes exactly how regression models are developed and evaluated. Real data are used, instead of contrived textbook-like problems. The data used in the book are the kind of data managers are faced with in the real world. Included are instructions for using Microsoft Excel to build business/economic models using regression analysis with an appendix using screen shots and step-by-step instructions.

Completing this book will allow you to understand and build basic business/economic models using regression analysis. You will be able to interpret the output of those models and you will be able to evaluate the models for accuracy and shortcomings. Even if you never build a model yourself, at some point in your career it is likely that you will find it necessary to interpret one; this book will make that possible.

Keywords

Regression analysis, ordinary least squares (OLS), time-series data, cross-sectional data, dependent variables, independent variables, point estimates, interval estimates, hypothesis testing, statistical significance, confidence level, significance level, p-value, R-squared, coefficient of determination, multicollinearity, correlation, serial correlation, seasonality, qualitative events, dummy variables, nonlinear regression models, market share regression model, Abercrombie & Fitch Co.

Contents

CHAPTER 1

Background Issues for Regression Analysis

Chapter 1 Preview

When you have completed reading this chapter you will:

- Realize that this is a practical guide to regression not a theoretical discussion.
- Know what is meant by cross-sectional data.
- Know what is meant by time-series data.
- Know to look for trend and seasonality in time-series data.
- Know about the three data sets that are used the most for examples in the book.
- Know how to differentiate between nominal, ordinal, interval, and ratio data.
- Know that you should use interval or ratio data when doing regression.
- Know how to access the "Data Analysis" functionality in Excel.

Introduction

The importance of the use of regression models in modern business and economic analysis can hardly be overstated. In this book, you will see exactly how such models can be developed. When you have completed the book you will understand how to construct, interpret, and evaluate regression models. You will be able to implement what you have learned by using "Data Analysis" in Excel to build basic mathematical models of business and economic relationships.

You will not know everything there is to know about regression; however, you will have a thorough understanding about what is possible and what to look for in evaluating regression models. You may not ever actually build such a model in your own work but it is very likely that you will, at some point in your career, be exposed to such models and be expected to understand models that someone else has developed.

Initial Data Issues

Before beginning to look at the process of building and evaluating regression models, first note that nearly all of the data used in the examples in this book are real data, not data that have been contrived to show some purely academic point. The data used are the kind of data one is faced with in the real world. Data that are used in business applications of regression analysis are either cross-sectional data or time-series data. We will use examples of both types throughout the text.

Cross-Sectional Data

Cross-sectional data are data that are collected across different observational units but in the same time period for each observation. For example, we might do a customer (or employee) satisfaction study in which we survey a group of people all at the same time (e.g., in the same month).

A cross-sectional data set that you will see in this book is one for which we gathered data about college basketball teams. In this data set, we have many variables concerning 82 college basketball teams **all for the same season**. The goal is to try to model what influences the conference winning percentage (WP) for such a team. You might think of this as a "production function" in which you want to know what factors will help produce a winning team.

Each of the teams represents one observation. For each observation, we have a number of potential variables that might influence (in a causal manner) a team's winning percent in their conference games. In Figure 1.1, you see a graph of the conference winning percentage for the 82 teams in the sample. These teams came from seven major sport conferences: ACC, Big 12, Big East, Big 10, Mountain West, PAC 10, and SEC.

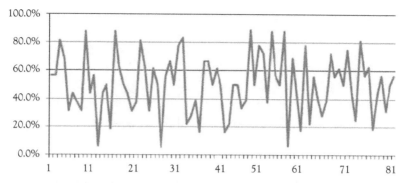

Figure 1.1 The conference winning percentage for 82 basketball teams: An example of cross-sectional data

Source: Statsheet at http://statsheet.com/mcb.

Time-series Data

Time-series data are data that are collected over time for some particular variable. For example, you might look at the level of unemployment by year, by quarter, or by month. In this book, you will see examples that use two primary sets of time-series data. These are women's clothing sales in the United States and the occupancy for a hotel.

A graph of the women's clothing sales is shown in Figure 1.2. When you look at a time-series graph, you should try to see whether you observe a trend (either up or down) in the series and whether there appears to be a regular seasonal pattern to the data. Much of the data that we deal with in business has either a trend or seasonality or both. Knowing this can be helpful in determining potential causal variables to consider when building a regression model.

The other time-series used frequently in the examples in this book is shown in Figure 1.3. This series represents the number of rooms occupied per month in a large independent motel. During the time period being considered, there was a considerable expansion in the number of casinos in the State, most of which had integrated lodging facilities. As you can see in Figure 1.3, there is a downward trend in occupancy. The owners wanted to evaluate the causes for the decline. These data are proprietary so the numbers are somewhat disguised as is the name of the hotel. But the data represent real business data and a real business problem.

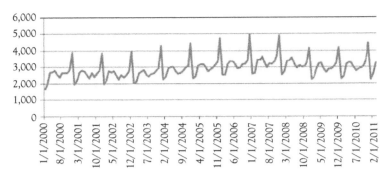

Figure 1.2 **Women's clothing sales per month in the United States in millions of dollars: An example of time-series data**

Source: www.economagic.com.

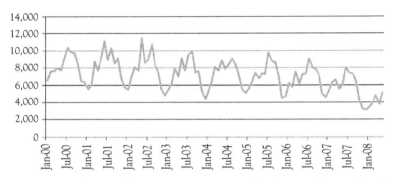

Figure 1.3 **Stoke's Lodge occupancy per month: A second example of time-series data.**

Source: Proprietary.

To help you understand regression analysis, these three sets of data will be discussed repeatedly throughout the book. Also, in Chapter 10, you will see complete examples of model building for quarterly Abercrombie & Fitch sales and quarterly U.S. retail jewelry sales (both time-series data). These examples will help you understand how to build regression models and how to evaluate the results.

An Additional Data Issue

Not all data are appropriate for use in building regression models. This means that before doing the statistical work of developing a regression model you must first consider what types of data you have. One way data are often classified is to use a hierarchy of four data types. These are: nominal, ordinal, interval, and ratio. In doing regression analysis, the data that you use should be composed of either interval or ratio numbers.[1] A short description of each will help you recognize when you have appropriate (interval or ratio) data for a regression model.

Nominal Data

Nominal data are numbers that simply represent a characteristic. The value of the number has no other meaning. Suppose, for example, that your company sells a product on four continents. You might code these continents as: 1 = Asia, 2 = Europe, 3 = North America, and 4 = South America. The numbers 1 through 4 simply represent regions of the world. Numbers could be assigned to continents in any manner. Some one else might have used different coding, such as: 1 = North America, 2 = Asia, 3 = South America, and 4 = Europe. Notice that arithmetic operations would be meaningless with these data. What would 1 + 2 mean? Certainly not 3! That is, Asia + Europe does not equal North America (based on the first coding above). And what would the average mean? Nothing, right? If the average value for the continents was 2.50 that number would be totally meaningless. With the exception of "dummy variables," never use nominal data in regression analysis. You will learn about dummy variables in Chapter 8.

Ordinal Data

Ordinal data also represent characteristics, but now the value of the number does have meaning. With ordinal data the number also represents some rank ordering. Suppose you ask someone to rank their top three fast food restaurants with 1 being the most preferred and 3 being the least preferred. One possible set of rankings might be:

$$1 = \text{Arby's}$$
$$2 = \text{Burger King}$$
$$3 = \text{Billy's Big Burger Barn (B}^4\text{)}$$

---

[1] There is one exception to this that is discussed in Chapter 8. The exception involves the use of a dummy variable that is equal to one if some event exists and zero if it does not exist.

From this you know that for this person Arby's is preferred to either Burger King or B[4]. But note that the distance between numbers is not necessarily equal. The difference between 1 and 2 may not be the same as the distance between 2 and 3. This person might be almost indifferent between Arby's and Burger King (1 and 2 are almost equal) but would almost rather starve than eat at B[4] (3 is far away from either 1 or 2). With ordinal or ranking data such as these arithmetic operations again would be meaningless. The use of ordinal data in regression analysis is not advised because results are very difficult to interpret.

Interval Data

Interval data have an additional characteristic in that the distance between the numbers is a constant. The distance between 1 and 2 is the same as the distance between 23 and 24, or any other pair of contiguous values. The Fahrenheit temperature scale is a good example of interval data. The difference between 32°F and 33°F is the same as the distance between 76°F and 77°F. Suppose that on a day in March the high temperature in Chicago is 32°F while the high in Atlanta is 64°F. One can then say that it is 32°F colder in Chicago than in Atlanta, or that it is 32°F warmer in Atlanta than in Chicago. Note, however, that we cannot say that it is twice as warm in Atlanta than in Chicago. The reason for this is that with interval data the zero point is arbitrary. To help you see this, note that a temperature of 0°F is not the same as 0°C (centigrade). At 32°F in Chicago it is also 0°C. Would you then say that in Atlanta it is twice as warm as in Chicago so it must be 0°C ($2 \times 0 = 0$) in Atlanta? Whoops, it doesn't work!

In business and economics, you may have survey data that you want to use. A common example is to try to understand factors that influence customer satisfaction. Often customer satisfaction is measured on a scale such as: 1 = very dissatisfied, 2 = somewhat dissatisfied, 3 = neither dissatisfied nor satisfied, 4 = somewhat satisfied, and 5 = very satisfied. Research has shown that it is reasonable to consider this type of survey data as interval data. You can assume that the distance between numbers is the same throughout the scale. This would be true of other scales used in survey data such as an agreement scale in which 1 = strongly agree to 5 = strongly disagree. The scales can be of various lengths such as 1–6 or 1–7 as well as the 5 point scales described previously. It is quite alright for you to use interval data in regression analysis.

Ratio Data

Ratio data have the same characteristics as interval data with one additional characteristic. With ratio data there is a true zero point rather than an arbitrary zero point. One way you might think about what a true zero point means is to think of zero as representing the absence of the thing that is being measured. For example, if a car dealer has zero sales for the day it means there were no sales. This is quite different from saying that 0°F means there is no temperature, or an absence of temperature.[2] Measures of income, sales, expenditures, unemployment rates, interest rates, population, and time are other examples of ratio data (as long as they have not been grouped into some set of categories). You can use ratio data in regression analysis. In fact, most of the data you are likely to use will be ratio data.

Finding "Data Analysis" in Excel

In Excel, sometimes the "Data Analysis" functionality does not automatically appear. But it is almost always available to you if you know where to look for it and how to make it available all the time. In Figures 1.4, 1.5, and 1.6, you will see how to activate "Data Analysis" in three different versions of Excel (Excel 2003, Excel 2007, and Excel 2010-2013, respectively). Figure 1.7 illustrates where "Data Analysis" shows up in the Excel Sheet under the data tab.

---

[2] There is a temperature scale, called the Kelvin scale, for which 0° does represent the absence of temperature. This is a very cold point at which molecular motion stops. Better bundle up.

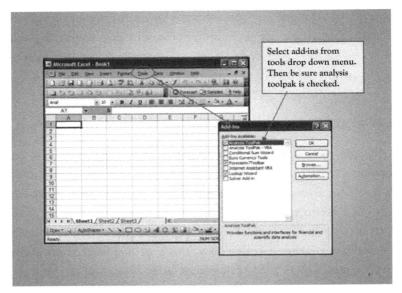

Figure 1.4 Getting "Data Analysis" in Excel 2003

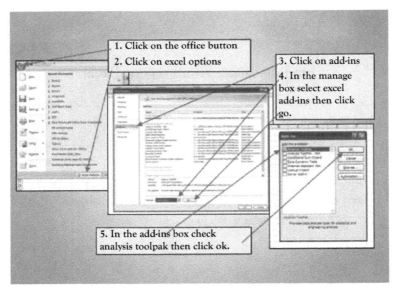

Figure 1.5 Getting "Data Analysis" in Excel 2007

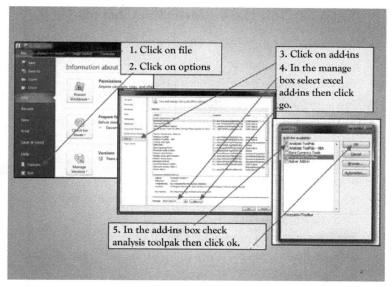

Figure 1.6 Getting "Data Analysis" in Excel 2010–2013

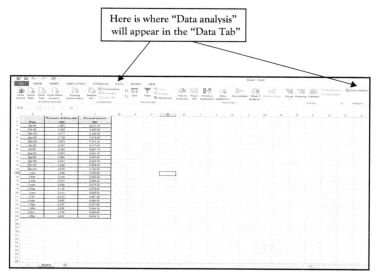

Figure 1.7 Where "Data Analysis" Now Shows Up in the Excel Sheet Under the Data Tab

What You Have Learned in Chapter 1

- You understand that this is a practical guide to regression, not a theoretical discussion.
- You know what is meant by cross-sectional data.
- You know what is meant by time-series data.
- You know to look for trend and seasonality in time-series data.
- You are familiar with the three data sets that are used for most of the examples in the remainder of the book.
- You know how to differentiate between nominal, ordinal, interval, and ratio data.
- You know that you should use interval or ratio data when doing regression (with the exception of "dummy variables"—see Chapter 8).
- You know how to access the "Data Analysis" functionality in Excel.

CHAPTER 2

Introduction to Regression Analysis

Chapter 2 Preview

When you have completed reading this chapter you will be able to:

- Understand what simple linear regression equations look like.
- See that you can form a general hypothesis (guess) about a relationship based on your knowledge of the situation being investigated.
- Know how to use a regression equation to make an estimate of the value of the variable you have modeled.
- See that line plots and scattergrams from Excel can be useful in using regression analysis.
- Understand how both time-series and cross-sectional data can be used in regression analysis.

Introduction

Regression analysis is a statistical tool that allows us to describe the way in which one variable is related to another. This description may be a simple one involving just two variables in a single equation, or it may be very complex, having many variables and even many equations, perhaps hundreds of each. From the simplest relationships to the most complex, regression analysis is useful in determining the way in which one variable is affected by one or more other variables. You will start to learn about the formal statistical aspects of regression in Chapter 3. However, before looking at formal models we will look at some examples to help you see the usefulness of regression in developing mathematical models.

One Example: Women's Clothing Sales

A relatively simple kind of model that can be specified using regression analysis is the relationship between some types of retail sales and personal income. We know from marketing and economics that retail sales of most (maybe all) products/services are dependent on the purchasing power of consumers. In the model used here you will see how personal income (a common measure of purchasing power) may influence the retail sales of women's clothing. The monthly level of women's clothing sales (in millions of dollars) is hypothesized to be a function of (depend on) the level of personal income (in billions of dollars).

When you construct such a hypothesis, you take the first step in building a model.[1] You must define the variables used in the model carefully so that the model can be tested and evaluated in a formal manner. Retail sales of women's clothing is a clearly defined statistical series that is published regularly, so there is little problem in defining that variable. The same can be said for personal income, which is regularly published in a number of places.[2] Both of these variables are examples of ratio data. For both variables, the distance between dollar amounts is constant no matter what the amounts are, and for both zero means the absence of that measure. We do not observe zero for either variable but zero would mean no sales or no income.

Women's Clothing Sales Data

To develop this model data for women's clothing sales, monthly data are used starting with January 2000 and continuing through March 2011. Thus, there are 135 values for each variable. Each of these 135 months represents one observation. It is not necessary to have this many observations but since all the calculations are performed in Excel you can use large data sets without any problem.[3] A shortened section of

---

[1] In Chapter 4, you will learn about the formal hypothesis test and how it is evaluated.

[2] The data used in this example come from the economagic.com website.

[3] One rule of thumb for the number of observations (sample size) is to have 10 times the number of independent (causal) variables. So, if you want to model sales as a function of income, the unemployment rate, and an interest rate you would need 30 observations (10×3). There is a mathematical constraint, but it is not usually relevant for business applications. There are times when this criterion cannot be met because of insufficient data.

the data is shown in Table 2.1. You see that each row represents an observation (24 observations in this shortened data set) and each column represents a variable (the date column plus two variables). It is common in a data file to use the first column for dates when using time-series data or for observation labels when using cross-sectional data. You will see a table of cross-sectional data for the basketball team's example in Table 2.2.

Table 2.1 *Monthly data for women's clothing sales and personal income (the first two years only, 2000 and 2001)*

Date	Women's clothing sales (M$)	Personal income (B$)
Jan-00	1,683	8,313.0
Feb-00	1,993	8,385.8
Mar-00	2,673	8,440.0
Apr-00	2,709	8,470.8
May-00	2,812	8,501.3
Jun-00	2,567	8,547.6
Jul-00	2,385	8,607.7
Aug-00	2,643	8,641.3
Sep-00	2,660	8,683.6
Oct-00	2,651	8,693.6
Nov-00	2,826	8,698.0
Dec-00	3,878	8,730.4
Jan-01	1,948	8,825.6
Feb-01	2,156	8,862.0
Mar-01	2,673	8,889.4
Apr-01	2,804	8,878.4
May-01	2,750	8,878.6
Jun-01	2,510	8,886.8
Jul-01	2,313	8,887.3
Aug-01	2,663	8,883.0
Sep-01	2,397	8,871.6
Oct-01	2,618	8,896.3
Nov-01	2,790	8,909.8
Dec-01	3,865	8,930.7

Source: economagic.com.

You know from Chapter 1 that the data shown in Table 2.1 are called *time-series data* because they represent values taken over a period of time for each of the variables involved in the model. In our example, the data are *monthly* time-series data. If you have a value for each variable by quarters, you would have a *quarterly* time series. Sometimes you might use values on a yearly basis, in which case your data would be an *annual* time series. The women's clothing sales data for the entire time period are shown graphically in Figure 2.1.

You notice in Figure 2.1 that women's clothing sales appears to have a seasonal pattern. Note the sharp peaks in the series that occur at regular intervals. These peaks are always in the month of December in each year. This seasonality is due to holiday shopping and gift giving, which you would expect to see for women's clothing sales. The dotted line added to the graph shows the long-term trend. You see that this trend is positive (slightly upward sloping). This means that over the period shown women's clothing sales have generally been increasing.

The Relationship between Women's Clothing Sales and Income

A type of graph known as a "scattergram" allows for a visual feel for the relationship between two variables. In a scattergram, the variable you are trying to model, or predict, is on the vertical (Y) axis (women's clothing sales) and the variable that you are using to help make a good prediction is on the horizontal (X) axis (personal income). Figure 2.2 shows the scattergram for this example.

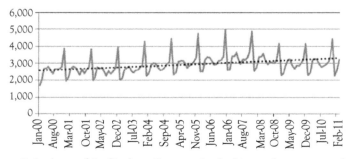

Figure 2.1 A graphic display of women's clothing sales per month (M\$). The dotted line represents the long-term trend in the sales data

You see that as income increases women's clothing sales also appear to increase. The solid line through the scatter of points illustrates this relationship. The majority of the observations lie within the oval represented by the dotted line. However, you do see some values that stand out above the oval. The relatively regular pattern of these observations that are outside the oval again suggest that there is seasonality in women's clothing sales.

Based on business/economic reasoning you might hypothesize that women's clothing sales would be related to the level of personal income. You would expect that as personal income increases sales would also increase. Such reasoning is certainly consistent with what you see in Figure 2.2. To state this relationship mathematically, you might write

$$WCS = f(PI)$$

where WCS represents women's clothing sales (measured in millions of dollars) and PI represents personal income (measured in billions of dollars). The business/economic assumption (or hypothesis) is that PI is influential in determining the level of WCS. For this reason, WCS is referred to as the dependent variable, while PI is the independent, or explanatory, variable.

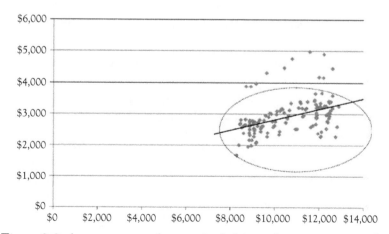

Figure 2.2 A scattergram of women's clothing sales versus personal income. Women's clothing sales (in M$) is on the vertical (Y) axis and personal income (in B$) is on the horizontal (X) axis

On the basis of the scatterplot in Figure 2.2, you might want to see whether a linear equation might fit these data well. You might be specific in writing the mathematical model as:

$$WCS = f(PI)$$
$$WCS = a + b(PI)$$

In the second form, you not only are hypothesizing that there is some functional relationship between WCS and PI but you are also stating that you expect the relationship to be linear. The obvious question you have now is: What are the appropriate values of a and b? Once you know these values, you will have made the model very specific. You can find the appropriate values for a and b using regression analysis.

Regression Results for Women's Clothing Sales

Using regression analysis for these data, you get the following mathematical relationship between women's clothing sales and personal income:

$$WCS = 1,187.123 + 0.165(PI)$$

If you put a value for personal income into this equation, you get an estimate of women's clothing sales for that level of personal income. Suppose that you want to estimate the dollar amount of women's clothing sales if personal income is 9,000 (billion dollars). You would have:

$$WCS = 1,187.123 + (0.165 \times 9,000)$$
$$WCS = 1,187.123 + 1,485 = 2,672.123$$

Thus, your estimate of woman's clothing sales if personal income is 9,000 (billion dollars) is $2,672.123 (million dollars) or $2,672,123,000.

If you were to put all 135 observations of personal income from the data into the aforesaid equation you would see how well this model does in predicting women's clothing sales at each of those income levels. You would find that personal income has a significant impact on women's clothing sales but that this model only explains about 17 percent of all the

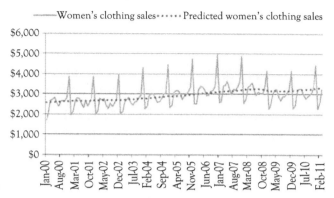

Figure 2.3 Women's clothing sales per month (M$) and values predicted based only on personal income

variation in women's clothing sales. It is likely that there are other variables that also have an influence on women's clothing sales. In Chapter 6, you will see that unemployment rate will be of some help in explaining more of the variation in those sales.

Figure 2.3 shows a graphic representation of the actual value of sales for each month along with the values predicted by the simple model used in this chapter. You see that this model fails to account for the seasonal peaks in the data. In Chapter 8, you will learn about a method to include the seasonality in the model and you will get much better predictions of monthly women's clothing sales. You will find that it is difficult to do a good job of modeling any business/economic activity using just one causal factor. However, using one causal variable is a good starting point to learn about regression analysis.

The simple model [WCS = 1,187.123 + 0.165(PI)] shows how women's clothing sales are related to personal income. Clearly, this model can be improved upon.

Another Example: Conference Winning Percentage for College Basketball Teams

What should a college basketball coach focus on when trying to put together a winning team? Given what many big time college basketball coaches earn, this is indeed a "million dollar" question. You may have seen the movie *MONEYBALL* in which "Data Analysis" was used to help a baseball team (the Oakland Athletics) improve their ability to win even though they had a low budget compared with other teams, such as the New York Yankees.[4] In the book and the movie, which was based on a real life situation, "Data Analysis" did indeed prove successful. The type of "Data Analysis" used in *MONEYBALL* was more advanced than regression analysis, but regression analysis is a good starting point and is the basis upon which the more advanced analyses are built.

Basketball Winning Percentage Data

Based on the basketball teams' data described in Chapter 1 you can create models using Excel to predict the winning percentage (WP) for college teams in the conferences represented in the data. Certainly, one factor you might think of as being important is the ability to make shots. From observing games, you could calculate the percentage of field goal (FG), attempts that are successful. Such data are available on the Internet.[5] Using these data, you can estimate the relationship between winning percentage (WP) and percentage of FGs made (FG).

The data used in this example are cross-sectional data because the data are all for the same season based on the results for 82 basketball teams from 7 major collegiate basketball conferences. The conferences, a sample of schools, and the two variables for those schools are shown in Table 2.2.

The range of WPs used for the schools in the data was from 5.6 percent to 88.9 percent. DePaul (5.6 percent) happened to have a bad conference year and Ohio State (88.9 percent) had a very good year. In that year, DePaul averaged 41.2 percent in FG percentage while Ohio State averaged 50 percent.

The Basketball Winning Percentage Regression Model

You might guess (hypothesize) that WP is determined, at least in part, by the percentage of FGs a team makes. Thus, you think perhaps:

$$WP = f(FG) \text{ or}$$
$$WP = a + b(FG)$$

---

[4] You may also read the book *MONEYBALL*, by Michael Lewis.
[5] See StatSheet at http://statsheet.com/mcb

Table 2.2 Conferences included in the data set, a representative school for each conference, and values of the variables for those schools

Conference	Team	Conference win %	Field goal %
ACC	Wake Forest	6.3	39.5
B12	Texas	81.3	45.6
Big East	Villanova	50.0	43.4
Big Ten	Wisconsin	72.2	44.5
Mountain West	UNLV	68.8	43.6
PAC 10	Arizona	77.8	46.5
SEC	South Carolina	31.3	37.1

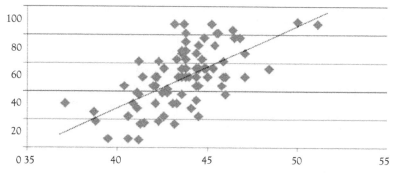

Figure 2.4 A scatterplot of winning percentage (vertical Y-axis) versus field goal percentage (horizontal X-axis). Note the X-axis has been scaled to go from 35% to 55% to better show the relationship

The scatterplot in Figure 2.4 helps you to see this relationship. As indicated by the dotted line through the observations, it appears that higher WPs are associated with higher percentages of FGs made. The equation for this relationship is obtained by using regression in Excel:

$$WP = -198.9 + 5.707(FG)$$

You see that there is a positive relationship between WP in conference games and the percentage of FGs completed. In fact, more detailed analysis of the results shows that about 40 percent of the variation in WP is explained by FG percentage. To a coach this probably seems obvious, but the analysis does provide support for using practice time to work on successful shooting of FGs.

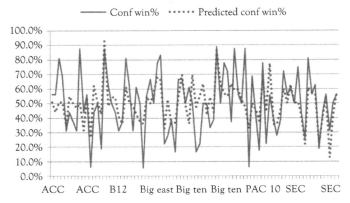

Figure 2.5 Actual conference winning percentage and the predicted winning percentage. The predictions are based on the regression model equation: WP = –198.9 + 5.707(FG)

In Figure 2.5, you see a graph which shows how well this regression model actually fits the original data. In this graph, the teams are arranged in conferences starting with the ACC and ending with the SEC. The solid line represents the actual WPs and the dotted line represents the WPs that would be predicted by the regression equation. While there are some big gaps overall it is not a bad model.

If you put a value of FG percentage into this equation you get an estimate of the team's WP for the season. Suppose that you want to estimate a team's WP if their FG percentage is 45 percent. You get:

$$WP = -198.9 + 5.707(FG)$$
$$WP = -198.9 + (5.707 \times 45) = 57.9$$

Thus, your estimate of a team's WP in their conference games if they make 45 percent of their FG attempts would be 57.9 percent.

A Warning about Applying a Regression Model

You should only use a regression model for values of the variables that are within, or close to being within, the range of values in your data set. Consider the basketball team's WP example. In the sample of data used to develop the regression model, the lowest FG goal percentage was

37.1 percent and the highest was 51.1 percent. Now suppose that you tried to estimate the conference WP of a team that had a FG success rate of 80 percent. You would get the following result:

$$WP = -198.9 + (5.707 \times 80) = 257.7$$

This would mean that this team would be predicted to win 257.7 percent of their games. This is clearly not possible. There are advanced forms of regression analysis that can constrain predictions to be no more than 100 percent. However, the most common type of regression analysis cannot do so. Thus, you need to be careful to only apply regression results within the scope of the data used to estimate your equation. The most common type of regression is called "ordinary least squares regression," which was used in this chapter and about which you will learn more in the next chapter.

Summary and Looking Ahead

In this chapter, you have started to get some feel for what regression analysis is all about. The examples should be viewed with a little skepticism because the models have not been evaluated to determine how good and how reasonable they really are. Nor have you learned how Excel gets the equations you have seen. In the next chapter, you will learn more about the statistical foundations of regression analysis. Then as you read through the rest of the book, you will build on your knowledge and understanding in each successive chapter. You will see how to evaluate regression models and how to expand beyond the use of only one causal variable.

What You Have Learned in Chapter 2

- You understand what simple linear regression equations look like.
- You see that you can form a general hypothesis (guess) about a relationship based on your knowledge of the situation being investigated.
- You know how to use a regression equation to make an estimate of the value of the variable you have modeled.

- You see that line plots and scattergrams from Excel can be useful in using regression analysis.
- You understand how both time-series and cross-sectional data can be used in regression analysis.
- You know to only apply a regression model for data within, or close to, the observations used to develop the model.

CHAPTER 3

The Ordinary Least Squares (OLS) Regression Model

Chapter 3 Preview

When you have completed reading this chapter you will be able to:

- Know the difference between a dependent variable and an independent variable.
- Know what portion of a regression equation (model) represents the intercept (or constant) and how to interpret that value.
- Know what part of the regression equation represents the slope and how to interpret that value.
- Know that for business applications the slope is the most important part of a regression equation.
- Know the ordinary least squares (OLS) criterion for the "best" regression line.
- Know four of the basic statistical assumptions underlying regression analysis.
- Know how to perform regression analysis in Excel.

The Regression Equation

In Chapter 2, you saw some examples of what is sometimes called "simple" linear regression. The term "simple" in this context means that only two variables are used in the regression. However, the mathematics and statistical foundation are not particularly simple. Two example regression equations discussed in Chapter 2 were:

1. Women's clothing sales (WCS) as a function of personal income (PI)

$$WCS = 1{,}187.123 + 0.165(PI)$$

2. Basketball team's conference winning percentage (WP) as a function of the team's successful field goal attempt percentage (FG)

$$WP = -198.9 + 5.707(FG)$$

In both of these regression equations, there are just two variables. While you use Excel to get these equations, the underlying mathematics can be relatively complex and certainly time consuming. Excel hides all those details from us and performs the calculations very quickly.

The Dependent (Y) and Independent Variables (X)

In the simplest form of regression analysis, you have only the variable you want to model (or predict) and one other variable that you hypothesize to have an influence on the variable you are modeling. The variable you are modeling (WCS or WP in the examples above) is called the **dependent variable**. The other variable (PI or FG) is called the **independent variable**. Sometimes the independent variable is called a "causal variable" because you are hypothesizing that this variable *causes* changes in the variable being modeled.

The dependent variable is often represented as Y, and the independent variable is represented as X. The relationship or model you seek to find could then be expressed as:

$$Y = a + b\,X$$

This is called a *bivariate* linear regression (BLR) model because there are just two variables: Y and X. Also, because both Y and X are raised to the first power the equation is linear.

The Intercept and the Slope

In the expression above, a represents the intercept or constant term for the regression equation. The intercept is where the regression line crosses the vertical, or Y, axis. Conceptually, it is the value that the dependent variable (Y) would have if the independent variable (X) had a value of zero. In this context, a is also called the constant because no matter what value bX has a is always the same, or constant. That is, as the independent variable (X) changes there is no change in a.

The value of b tells you the slope of the regression line. The slope is the rate of change in the dependent variable for each unit change in the independent variable. Understanding that the slope term (b) is the rate of change in Y as X changes will be helpful to you in interpreting regression results. If b has a positive value, Y increases when X increases and Y decreases when X decreases. On the other hand, if b is negative, Y changes in the opposite direction of changes in X. The slope (b) is the most important part of the regression equation, or model, for business decisions.

The Slope and Intercept for Women's Clothing Sales

You might think about a and b in the context of the two examples you have seen so far. First, consider the women's clothing sales model:

$$\text{WCS} = 1{,}187.123 + 0.165(\text{PI})$$

In this model, a is 1,187.123 million dollars. Conceptually, this means if personal income in the United States drops to zero women's clothing sales would be \$1,187,128,000. However, from a practical perspective you realize this makes no sense. If no one has any income in the United States you would not expect to see over a billion dollars being spent on women's clothing. Granted there is the theoretical possibility that even with no income people could draw on savings for such spending, but the reality of this happening is remote. It is equally remote that personal income would drop to zero.

Figure 2.2 is reproduced here as Figure 3.1. The line drawn through the scattergram represents the regression equation for these data. You see that the regression line would cross the Y-axis close to the intercept value of \$1,187.123 if extended that far from the observed data. You also see that the origin ($Y = 0$ and $X = 0$) is very far from the observed values of the data.

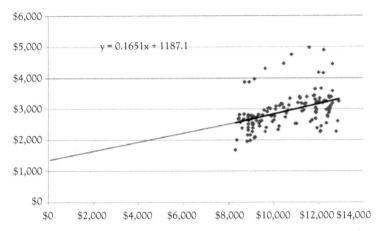

Figure 3.1 Scattergram of women's clothing sales versus personal income. Women's clothing sales is on the vertical (Y) axis and personal income is on the horizontal (X) axis[1]

The slope, or *b*, in the women's clothing sales example is 0.165. This means that for every one unit increase in personal income women's clothing sales would be estimated to increase by 0.165 units. In this example, personal income is in billions of dollars and women's clothing sales is in millions of dollars. Therefore, a one billion dollar increase in personal income would increase women's clothing sales by 0.165 million dollars ($165,000).

The Slope and Intercept for Basketball Winning Percentage

For the basketball WP model discussed in Chapter 2, the model is:

$$WP = -198.9 + 5.707(FG)$$

In this example, the intercept *a* is negative (–198.9). Because the intercept just positions the height of the line in the graph, and because

---

[1] The equation written in the scattergram is the way you would get it from Excel. In this format, the slope times the independent variable is the first term and the intercept or constant is the second term. Mathematicians often use this form but the way the equation is presented in this book is far more common in practice. By comparing the two forms of the function you can see they give the same result.

the origin is usually outside of the range of relevant data whether the intercept is positive, negative, or zero is usually of no concern. It is just a constant to be used when applying the regression model. It certainly cannot be interpreted in this case that if a team had a zero success rate for FG attempts the percentage of wins would be negative.

For the slope term the interpretation is very useful. The number 5.707 tells you that for every 1 percent increase in the percentage of FGs that are made the team's WP would be estimated to increase by about 5.7 percent. Similarly, a drop of 1 percent in FG would cause the WP to fall by about 5.7 percent. This knowledge could be very useful to a basketball coach. In later chapters, you will see how other independent variables can affect the WP of basketball teams.

How Can You Determine the Best Regression Line for Your Data?

The most commonly used criterion for the "best" regression line is that the sum of the squared vertical differences between the observed values and the estimated regression line be as small as possible. To illustrate this concept, Figure 3.2 shows five observations of the relationship between some Y variable and some X variable. You can see from the scattering of points that no straight line would go through all of the points. You would

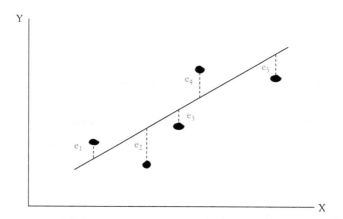

Figure 3.2 The ordinary least squares regression line for Y as a function of X. Residuals (or deviations or errors) between each point and the regression line are labeled e$_i$

like to find the one line that does the "best" job of fitting the data. Thus, there needs to be a common and agreed upon criterion for what is best.

This criterion is to **minimize the sum of the squared vertical deviations of the observed values from the regression line**. This is called "ordinary least squares" (OLS) regression.

The vertical distance between each point and the regression line is called a deviation.[2] Each of these deviations is indicated by e_i (where the subscript i refers to the number of the observation). A regression line is drawn through the points in Figure 3.2. The deviations between the actual data points and the estimates made from the regression line are identified as e_1, e_2, e_3, e_4, and e_5. Note that some of the deviations are positive (e_1 and e_4), while the others are negative (e_2, e_4, and e_5). Some errors are fairly large (such as e_2), while others are small (such as e_3).

By our criterion, the best regression line is that line which minimizes the sum of the squares of these deviations (min $\Sigma(e_i)^2$). This regression method (OLS) is the most common type of regression. If someone says they did a regression analysis you can assume it was OLS regression unless some other method is specified. In OLS regression, the deviations are squared so that positive and negative deviations do not cancel each other out as we find their sum. The single line that gives us the smallest sum of the squared deviations from the line is the best line according to the OLS method.

An Example of OLS Regression Using Annual Values of Women's Clothing Sales

The annual values for women's clothing sales (AWCS) are shown in Table 3.1. To get a linear trend over time, you can use regression with AWCS as a function of time. Usually time is measured with an index starting at 1 for the first observation. In Table 3.1, the heading for this column is "Year."

---

[2] The deviations from the regression line (e_i) are also frequently called residuals or errors. You are likely to see the term residuals used in printouts from some computer programs that perform regression analysis, such as in Excel.

Table 3.1 Annual data for women's clothing sales with regression trend predictions. This OLS model results in some negative and some positive errors which should be expected[3]

Date	Year	AWCS (annual data)	Trend predictions for AWCS (annual data)	Error (actual–predicted)
2000	1	31,480	31,483	−3
2001	2	31,487	32,257	−770
2002	3	31,280	33,031	−1,751
2003	4	32,598	33,805	−1,207
2004	5	34,886	34,579	307
2005	6	37,000	35,353	1,647
2006	7	38,716	36,127	2,589
2007	8	40,337	36,901	3,436
2008	9	38,351	37,675	676
2009	10	35,780	38,449	−2,669
2010	11	36,969	39,223	−2,254

The OLS regression equation for the women's clothing sales trend on an annual basis (AWCS) is shown in Figure 3.3. The OLS regression equation is[4]:

$$AWCS = 30,709.200 + 773.982(Year)$$

In Figure 3.3, you see that for 2000 the model is almost perfect, having a very small error and that the error is the largest for 2007. Overall, the dotted line showing the predicted values is the "best" regression line using the OLS criterion.

---

[3] You should enter the data in Table 3.1 into Excel and use it for practice with regression. You can compare your results with those shown here.

[4] This type of regression model is often called a trend regression. Some people would call the independent variable "Time" rather than "Year."

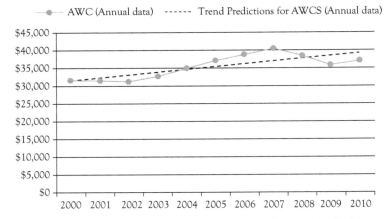

Figure 3.3 The OLS regression trend for annual women's clothing sales (M$). Here you see that for 2000, the regression trend was almost perfect and that the biggest error is for 2007

The Underlying Assumptions of the OLS Regression Model

There are certain mathematical assumptions that underlie the OLS regression model. To become an expert in regression you would want to know all of these, but our goal is not to make you an expert. The goal is to help you be an informed user of regression, not a statistical expert. However, there are four of these assumptions that you should be familiar with in order to appreciate both the power and the limitations of OLS regression.

The Probability Distribution of Y for Each X

First for each value of an independent variable (*X*) there is a probability distribution of the dependent variable (*Y*). Figure 3.4 shows the probability distributions of *Y* for two of the possible values of *X* (X_1 and X_2). The means of the probability distributions are assumed to lie on a straight line, according to the equation: $Y = a + bX$. In other words, the mean value of the dependent variable is assumed to be a linear function of the independent variable (note that the regression line in Figure 3.4 is directly under the peaks of the probability distributions for *Y*).

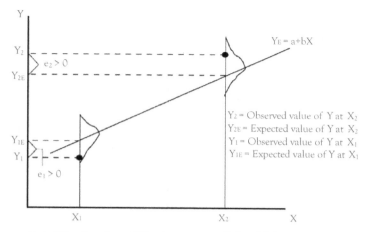

Figure 3.4 Distribution of Y values around the OLS regression line.
For any X, the possible values of Y are assumed to be distributed
normally around the regression line. Further, the errors or residuals
(e_i) are assumed to be normally distributed with a mean of zero and a
constant standard deviation

The Dispersion of Y for Each X

Second, OLS assumes that the standard deviation of each of the probability distributions is the same for all values of the independent variable (such as X_1 and X_2). In Figure 3.4, the "spread" of both of the probability distributions shown is the same (this characteristic of equal standard deviations is called homoscedasticity).

Values of Y are Independent of One Another

Third, the values of the dependent variable (Y) are assumed to be independent of one another. If one observation of Y lies below the mean of its probability distribution, this does not imply that the next observation will also be below the mean (or anywhere else in particular).

The Probability Distribution of Errors Follow a Normal Distribution

Fourth, the probability distributions of the errors, or residuals, are assumed to be normal. That is, the differences between the actual values of Y and the expected values (from the regression line) are normally distributed random variables with a mean of zero and a constant standard deviation.

Theory versus Practice

These four assumptions may be viewed as the ideal to which one aspires when using regression. While these underlying assumptions of regression are sometimes violated in practice, they should be followed closely enough to ensure that estimated regression equations represent true relationships between variables. For the practitioner, it is important to note that if these four assumptions are not at least closely approximated, the resulting OLS regression analysis may be flawed. Summary statistics that are used with regression analysis allow us to check compliance with these assumptions. These statistics are described later, as are the likely outcomes of violating these assumptions.

Doing Regression in Excel

To do regression analysis in Excel, you need to use the "Data Analysis" tools of Excel. How you get to "Data Analysis" depends on the version of Excel you are using. The instructions to get to "Data Analysis" are given at the end of Chapter 1. Once you get to the "Data Analysis" dialog box, the process of doing regression is the same in all versions of Excel. What follows is based on screen shots for Excel 2013 but the process within "Data Analysis" will work in all versions of Excel.

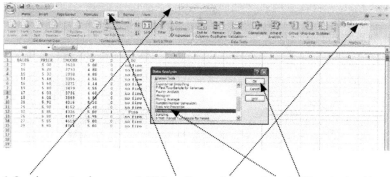

1. Start by entering data or opening a data file. Here, an example file is opened.

2. Click on Data and then select "Data Analysis".

3. In the "Data Analysis" box select Regression.

4. Then click on OK.

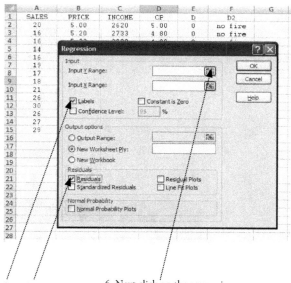

5. Check labels and residuals

6. Next click on the square in the Input Y Range box.

Then, drag over the range for the Y (dependent) variable(s). This is shown below. You see that the column for sales has a dashed line around it to indicate it has been selected and the range is shown in the small dialog box. To complete the selection of Y click here.

7. Next click on the square in the Input X Range box, which is right below the Input Y Range box.

Then, drag over the range for the X (independent) variable(s). If you have more than one independent variable they should be in adjacent columns. This is shown below. You see that the columns for price, income, CP, and D have a dashed line around them to indicate they have been selected and the range is shown in the dialog box. Sometimes you may need to move columns around a bit so that all independent variables are in contiguous columns.

To complete the selection
of the X variables click here.

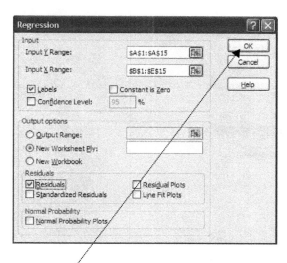

This brings you back to the main regression dialog box. You are now ready for Excel to calculate the regression equations so click on OK.

The results will appear on a new sheet, as shown below. You will probably want to delete some of this output and reformat the column widths and cells, especially reducing the number of decimal points shown.

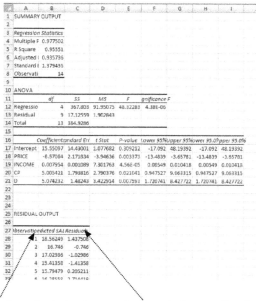

You can copy the predicted values then paste them in a column next to your original Y values to make it easy to generate a graph and to illustrate how the actual and predicted values compare.

For time series data, you will need to program in the Durbin–Watson formula. The Residuals column contains the necessary data (the residuals are often called the errors). The Durbin–Watson formula is given in Chapter 4.

To obtain the correlation coefficients for the independent variables:

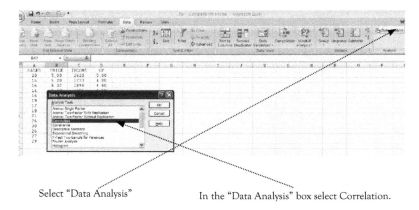

Select "Data Analysis"   In the "Data Analysis" box select Correlation.

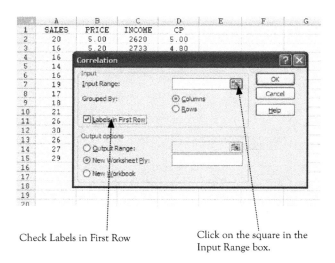

Check Labels in First Row   Click on the square in the
                                     Input Range box.

Then, drag over the range for the independent variables. This is shown below. You see that the columns for price, income, and CP have a dashed line around them to indicate they have been selected and the range is shown in the dialog box. Then click here.

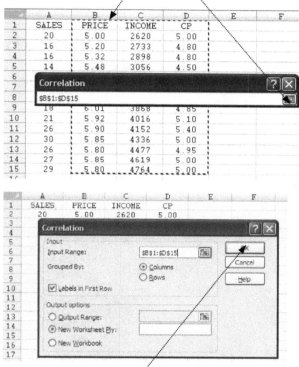

This brings you back to the main Correlation dialog box. You are now ready for Excel to calculate the correlation coefficients so click on OK.

The results will appear on a new sheet, as shown below.

	A	B	C	D
1		*PRICE*	*INCOME*	*CP*
2	PRICE	1		
3	INCOME	0.794293	1	
4	CP	0.165771	0.477671	1

What You Have Learned in Chapter 3

- You know the difference between a dependent variable and an independent variable.
- You know what portion of a regression equation (model) represents the intercept (or constant) and how to interpret that value.
- You know what part of the regression equation represents the slope and how to interpret that value.
- You know that for business applications the slope is the more important part of a regression equation.
- You know the ordinary least squares (OLS) criterion for the "best" regression line.
- You know four of the basic statistical assumptions underlying regression analysis.
- You know how to perform regression analysis in Excel.

CHAPTER 4

Evaluation of Ordinary Least Squares (OLS) Regression Models

Chapter 4 Preview

When you have completed reading this chapter you will be able to:

- Identify the four steps involved in evaluating a simple regression model.
- Evaluate whether a simple regression model makes logical sense.
- Check for statistical significance of a slope term.
- Identify when it is appropriate to use a one-tailed versus a two-tailed hypothesis test.
- Evaluate the explanatory power of a simple regression model.
- Check for serial correlation in simple regression models based on time-series data.

Introduction

At this point, you are familiar with the basics of OLS regression analysis and how to perform it in Excel. In this chapter, you will learn a relatively simple process that will help you to evaluate OLS regression models. These could either be regressions that you have developed or they might be models that you obtained from elsewhere. The evaluation process for simple regression can be summarized by a set of four questions that you should ask yourself as you look at a regression model. These are:

1. Does the model make sense? That is, is it consistent with a logical view of the situation being investigated?
2. Is there a statistically significant relationship between the dependent and the independent variable?

3. What percentage of the variation in the dependent variable does the regression model explain?

4. Is there a problem of serial correlation among the error terms in the model?

Let us now consider each of these questions and how they can be answered.

Evaluation Step 1: Evaluate Whether the Model Makes Sense

First and foremost, your model should be logical. Something is likely wrong if the results of your regression are at odds with what reasonable logic would suggest. You should not proceed to the remaining steps of the evaluation process if the model does not make sense. For example, consider the following regression model that investigates the influence that product price (P) has on unit sales (S):

$$S = 240 + 1.22(P)$$

Does this model make sense? The value of the slope on price is positive indicating that if price increases then unit sales will also increase. Should you go to management and tell them if they want to increase unit sales that they should just raise their price? And, if the initial price increase does not increase sales enough to just keep increasing price because there is a positive relationship between price and sales? Certainly not. This illogical result indicates that something is wrong with the model. There is strong economic and business logic (as well as considerable empirical evidence) that supports the notion that unit sales and price are inversely related in nearly all cases. Thus, we should expect that the sign for the slope would be negative. When the sign of the slope term is not what logic would suggest the model does not make sense and should not be used.

The situation discussed above is not an uncommon finding when regressing unit sales on price.[1] You will see a similar example of this when

---

[1] If sales were measured in dollars, the slope could be either positive or negative depending on the price elasticity of demand. It would be positive for an inelastic demand and negative for an elastic demand.

evaluating market share in Chapter 7. What is the problem that leads to such an illogical result? In this case, the problem is that the model is probably *underspecified*, meaning that there are additional factors that have not been considered in the model that have caused sales to go up despite price increases rather than because of price increases. For example, perhaps incomes have also increased, or the size of the market has expanded due to a relaxation in international trade barriers, or greater advertising has increased product demand. In Chapter 6, you will learn about multiple regression analysis and see how other such factors can easily be incorporated into the model.

Unfortunately, there is no statistic that you can evaluate or no formal test that you can perform to determine whether or not the model makes sense. You must do that yourself based on your understanding of the relationship being modeled. If you cannot make the correct judgment about the appropriate sign you probably do not know enough about the area of investigation to be working with the model.

Let's consider the basketball WP model discussed in Chapter 2. What expectation do you have about the relationship between the team's winning percentage (WP) and the percentage of field goals made (FG)? The more FG attempts that are successful, the more points the team should score, making them more likely to win games and have a higher WP. Thus, we should expect to see a positive sign on the slope term in the model. The OLS equation was found to be:

$$WP = -198.9 + 5.707(FG)$$

We see the sign is indeed positive and so this model does make sense.

Evaluation Step 2: Check for Statistical Significance

Background to Help Guide Your Thinking

Suppose that you ask 24 people to each give you the first number that comes to their mind. Then you split the 24 numbers into two sets of 12, calling one set Y and the other set X. An example can be seen in Table 4.1.

Next, you enter these data into Excel and regress Y on X; that is, Y as a function of X. You would get an intercept and a slope. But, would the

Table 4.1 Twenty-four arbitrary numbers split into X and Y

Y	14	19	10	14	9	18	20	13	8	19	14	16
X	5	6	7	10	13	13	13	15	18	18	21	21

regression equation have any useful meaning? Would you expect to find a functional relationship between Y and X? You no doubt answered no to both of these questions. That is, if the values of X and Y are selected in such an arbitrary manner, you would not expect to find a functional relationship between them.

If Y is not a function of X, it means that Y does not depend on X and that the best estimate of Y is the mean of Y, regardless of the value of X. If Y is not a function of X, it means that changes in X do not result in a change in Y. If this is the case, the regression line would have a slope equal to zero ($b = 0$). The scattergram in Figure 4.1 illustrates such a case for the data shown in Table 4.1.

The OLS regression equation for the set of points in Table 4.1 is given by:

$$Y = 14.66 - 0.012(X)$$

Notice that the intercept value of 14.66 in the regression equation is very close to the mean value of Y which is 14.5. In fact, if you draw the regression line in Figure 4.1, you will find that it is very close to the horizontal line already drawn at the mean of Y.

You also see that the slope is -0.012. Is this number close to zero or far from zero? Actually, the answer is that we do not know. We cannot determine the answer by just looking at the value of b. For any such number we cannot leave it to an individual's judgment because that could lead to disagreements rather than a clear answer. Thus, we need a statistical answer for which there would be universal agreement.

So, it is necessary to use a statistical method of evaluating regression equations to determine if there is a meaningful functional relationship between Y and X. This can be accomplished by performing a formal statistical hypothesis test called the "*t*-test." A *t*-test is used to see if the estimated slope (b) is statistically different from zero. If it is, there is sufficient evidence in the data to support the existence of a functional

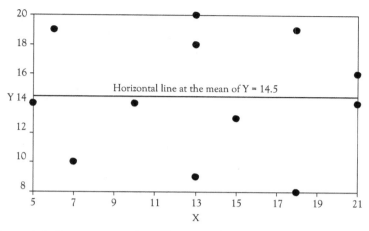

Figure 4.1 *Scattergram when* X *is not a function of* Y. *The solid line represents the mean value of* Y. *When no relationship exists, the best estimate of* Y *for any observed value of* X *is the mean value of* Y *(represented by the solid line)*

relationship between Y and X and you say that the slope (b) is, in fact, statistically significant. On the other hand, if the estimated slope (b) is not statistically different from zero, then you conclude that Y is not a linear function of X.

In hypothesis testing, sample statistics are used to make conclusions about unknown population parameters. For regression, you collect a sample of data and run a regression and obtain a slope term that tells you about the relationship between Y and X for your sample of data. Therefore, b is the sample statistic. However, you are really interested in the true functional relationship between Y and X for all possible values (the entire population) of Y and X. The true relationship between Y and X, referred to as β, is the unknown population parameter. Usually, you do not have enough time or money to find all possible values of Y and X *or* there might be an infinite number of values. So, as an alternative, you use your sample statistic *(b)* to draw conclusions about the unknown population parameter *(β)*. This is where the t-test comes in.

The Formal Hypothesis Test: Three Possibilities

Every hypothesis test contains a null and alternative hypothesis. The null hypothesis (H_0) is the proposition that implies that there is **not** a relationship that is consistent with your business/economic assumption or reasoning. The alternative, or research, hypothesis (H_1) states what you are statistically trying to test. For this reason H_1 is often called the "research hypothesis."

The statistical test of significance of a regression slope (sometimes referred to as a coefficient) can take any of the following three forms depending on what you are trying to determine (i.e., what the business/economic reasoning suggests is logical).

Case 1: This form is appropriate when you are simply testing for the existence of *any* linear functional relationship between Y and X. In this case, you have no *a priori* belief as to whether the slope will be positive or negative. You start out assuming that the true relationship between Y and X is zero (null hypothesis). Then, based on your sample, determine if you can conclude statistically that the true relationship between Y and X is nonzero (alternative hypothesis) which implies the existence of a linear relationship between Y and X.

$$H_0 : \beta = 0$$
$$H_1 : \beta \neq 0$$

Case 2: This form is appropriate if you think that the relationship between Y and X is an inverse one. That is, you would use this form when you expect an increase (decrease) in X to cause a decrease (increase) in Y. In this case, you start by assuming that the true relationship between Y and X is greater than or equal to zero (null hypothesis). Then statistically, based on your sample, determine if you can conclude that the true relationship between Y and X is negative (alternative hypothesis), which implies the existence of an inverse linear relationship between Y and X.

$$H_0 : \beta \geq 0$$
$$H_1 : \beta < 0$$

Case 3: This form is appropriate if you think that the relationship between Y and X is a direct one. That is, you would use this form when you expect an increase (decrease) in X to cause an increase (decrease) in Y. In this case, you start by assuming that the true relationship between

Y and X is less than or equal to zero (null hypothesis). Then statistically, based on your sample, determine if you can conclude that the true relationship between Y and X is positive (alternative hypothesis), which implies the existence of a direct linear relationship between Y and X.

$$H_0 : \beta \leq 0$$
$$H_1 : \beta > 0$$

In all three cases described so far, the goal is to determine whether statistically there is enough evidence to reject the null hypothesis in favor of the alternative (research) hypothesis. If you can reject the null hypothesis you have enough statistical evidence that the slope or coefficient is statistically significant. That is, you need to determine if your sample slope (b) is statistically far enough away from zero to conclude that the true population slope (β) is either different than zero (Case 1), less than zero (Case 2), or greater than zero (Case 3). The critical value of a hypothesis test tells you how "far away" from zero your sample slope must be in order for the estimated slope (b) to be significant. This hypothesis test is called the "t-test" because it is based on the Student's t-distribution and therefore you need to use a t-table (see Appendix 4B) in order to find the appropriate critical value.

Examples of Applying the Hypothesis Tests

As an analyst, you must make an important decision before you can proceed to find the critical value. You must decide upon your desired level of confidence in decision making. Once you decide upon your required level of confidence, it provides you with a related measure which is the level of significance and is denoted by α. The level of confidence and the level of significance must sum to 100 percent or 1.0 (in decimal form). Therefore, if the level of confidence is 95 percent, then the level of significance is 5 percent or $\alpha = 0.05$.[2]

---

[2] A 95 percent level of confidence is common. However, 90 percent and 99 percent are also used at times.

In performing a *t*-test, you not only have to decide on a level of confidence, but you also have to correctly identify the number of degrees of freedom (df) to use. In simple linear regression, the appropriate number of degrees of freedom is: df = *n* − 2, where *n* equals the number of observations used in the sample to determine the values of the intercept (*a*) and slope (*b*) and 2 is the number of parameters estimated (*a* and *b*).[3]

You can next calculate the computed test statistic or *t*-ratio (t_c) in order to determine how far (in terms of "statistical" distance) your sample slope is from zero:

$$t_c = \frac{b - 0}{\text{SE of } b}$$

where SE of *b* is the standard error of *b* (the standard deviation of the probability distribution of the estimator *b*). The standard error is included in the output of virtually all regression programs. In Excel, it is given in the column adjacent to the slope coefficient. The value of t_c indicates how many standard errors the estimate of *β* (the sample slope, *b*) is from zero. The larger the absolute value of the *t*-ratio, the more confident you can be that the true value of *β* is not zero and that *Y* is in fact a linear function of *X*. Most regression programs also give the calculated *t*-statistic (t_c) as a standard part of the regression output. In Excel, it is given in the column next to the standard error of *b* and labeled "*t*-stat." You are now ready to find the critical *t*-table value and then compare it with the computed test statistic, t_c, in order to determine your statistical conclusion.

Application of Case 1.   Situations such as that described in Case 1 require the use of a two-tailed test because you are trying to determine if the slope is *either* significantly higher *or* significantly lower (different) than zero. Therefore, the level of significance (α) must be split between the two tails of the *t*-distribution. That is, $\frac{\alpha}{2}$ is the area under each tail of the

---

[3] For more information about degrees of freedom see Appendix 4A: More Details Concerning the Concept of "Degrees of Freedom."

t-distribution. This means that if you want to have a 95 percent confidence level, you would have to find the critical values that put a probability of 2.5 percent of the total area under the t-distribution in the outer part of each tail of the t-distribution, as illustrated in Figure 4.2.

The critical values define what is known as the rejection region. For a two-tailed test, the null hypothesis is rejected if the absolute value of t_c is greater than or equal to the critical t-table value at the desired confidence level. That is, t_c lies in either the lower or upper shaded tail of the t-distribution.

Reconsider the data presented in Table 4.1. The values of X and Y were selected in such an arbitrary manner that you would not have any expectation about the direction of the relationship between Y and X. So, you would just be testing whether the estimated slope was indeed statistically significantly *different* from zero, which implies that there is linear relationship between Y and X. Therefore, a two-tailed test would be appropriate. Recall that the regression equation for that data is:

$$Y = 14.66 - 0.012(X)$$

The null hypothesis is that the slope is equal to zero ($H_0 : \beta = 0$). The alternative hypothesis is that the slope is not equal to zero ($H_1 : \beta \neq 0$).

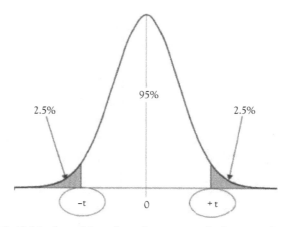

Figure 4.2 Critical t-table values for a two-tailed test with a 95 percent level of confidence. The values for "+t" and "–t" are obtained from a t-table with df = n – 2

Excel results showed that the standard error of b for this regression is 0.231, so we can calculate t_c as follows:

$$t_c = \frac{b-0}{SE \text{ of } b} = \frac{-0.012-0}{0.231} = -0.052$$

There were 12 observations in the data set, so the number of degrees of freedom is: df $= n - 2 = 12 - 2 = 10$. From the t-table in Appendix 4B, find the row for 10 degrees of freedom and the column for a two-tailed test with a level of significance of 0.05, and you find the critical value for t to be 2.228 (appropriate columns for the two-tailed tests are defined along the bottom of the table in Appendix 4B). Thus, in this case the absolute value of t_c ($|-0.052|$) is not greater than the critical table value (2.228) and you do not have enough statistical evidence to reject the null. Therefore, you conclude that there is not a statistically significant relationship between Y and X at the 5 percent level of significance ($\alpha = 0.05$).

Applications of Cases 2 and 3.   On the other hand, situations such as those described in Cases 2 and 3 call for the use of a one-tailed test because you are only trying to determine if the slope is below zero (Case 2) *or* above zero (Case 3). Therefore, the entire level of significance (α) goes in either the outer part of the lower tail or the upper tail of the t-distribution. This means that if you want to be 95 percent confident, then you would have the entire 5 percent significance level in the outer part of either the lower tail (Case 2) or upper tail (Case 3) of the t-distribution. The number of degrees of freedom is still equal to $n - 2$.

Situations described in Case 2 require the use of a left-tailed test. The null hypothesis is rejected and you conclude that the true slope is negative if t_c is less than or equal to the negative critical t-table value ($-t$) at the desired confidence level.[4] Similarly, situations described in Case 3 require the use of a right-tailed test. The null hypothesis is rejected and you conclude that the true slope is positive if t_c is greater than or equal to the positive critical t-table value ($+t$) at the desired confidence level. The appropriate rejection region for each case is illustrated in Figure 4.3.

----

[4] Mathematically, this is the same as rejecting the null if the absolute value of the computed test statistic ($|t_c|$) is greater than the positive critical t-table value ($+t$).

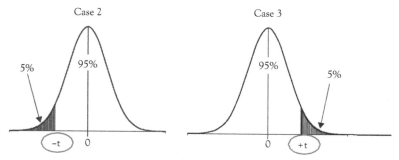

Figure 4.3 *Critical t-table values for one-tailed tests with a 95 percent level of confidence. The values for "+t" and "–t" are obtained from a t-table with df = n – 2*

Now let's check the statistical significance of the basketball WP model developed earlier. You have already determined that the model makes sense because the slope term is positive (as FG percentage increases, WP also increases). But, is the slope statistically significantly greater than zero? This calls for a one-tailed test of the type described in Case 3. The information we need to perform the test is described in the box below:

The regression equation is: WP = –198.9 + 5.707(FG)

$$n = 82 \text{ so df} = 82 - 2 = 80$$

Computer results show that the standard error of b is: 0.783

Using a 95 percent confidence level (a 5 percent significance level) the t-table value (from Appendix 4B) is: 1.671 *(Always use the row that is closest to your actual df.)*

$$H_0 : \beta \le 0; \text{ slope is less than or equal to zero}$$
$$H_1 : \beta > 0; \text{ slope is greater than zero}$$

The computed test statistic or t-ratio, t_c, can be calculated as follows:

$$t_c = \frac{b - 0}{\text{SE of } b} = \frac{5.707 - 0}{0.783} = 7.286$$

The t_c (7.286) is greater than the critical t-table value (1.671). Thus, the calculated t-ratio would be out in the rejection region or shaded portion of the right-hand tail of the t-distribution and the null hypothesis is rejected. As a result, the slope is statistically significant! That is, at a 95 percent confidence level there is enough statistical evidence to show that WP is positively related to FG percentage (for the population of collegiate basketball teams).

A rule of thumb is often used in evaluating t-ratios when a t-table is not handy. The rule is that the slope term is likely to be significantly different from zero if the absolute value of the calculated t-ratio is greater than 2. This is a handy rule to remember.

Evaluation Step 3: Determine the Explanatory Power of the Model

The dependent variable (Y) used in a regression analysis will have some variability. Otherwise, there would be no reason to try to model Y. It would be convenient to have a measure of how much of that variation in Y is explained by the regression model. This is where the coefficient of determination (R^2) comes in handy.

The **coefficient of determination (R^2)** *gives the percentage of the variation in the dependent variable (Y) that is explained by the regression model.* The worst possible explanatory power a model could have is to explain none of the variation in the dependent variable ($R^2 = 0$), and the best possible model would be one that explains all of the variations in the dependent variable ($R^2 = 1.0$). Hence, the coefficient of determination (R^2) will always be a value between 0 and 1. The closer it is to 0 the lower the explanatory power of the model, while the closer it is to 1 the greater is the explanatory power of the model.

For the basketball WP model the coefficient of determination is 0.399.[5] This means that 39.9 percent of the variation in WP (the dependent variable) is explained by the model. Or you could say, 39.9 percent of the variation in WP is explained by the variation in FG percentage (the independent variable).

Evaluation Step 4: Check for Serial Correlation

As mentioned earlier, many business and economic applications of regression analysis rely on the use of time-series data. You have already

---

[5] One would rarely calculate the coefficient of determination manually. It will generally be given in the computer printout and is most often identified as "R-Squared" or "R²" (in Excel it is R-Square).

seen an example of such an application in the estimation of women's clothing sales. When time-series data are used a problem known as serial correlation can occur.

One of the assumptions of the OLS regression model is that the error terms are normally distributed random variables with a mean of zero and a constant variance (see Chapter 3). If this is true, we would not expect to find any regular pattern in the error terms. When a significant time pattern is found in the error terms, serial correlation is indicated.

Figure 4.4 illustrates the two possible cases of serial correlation. In the left-hand graph, the case of negative serial correlation is apparent. Perfect negative serial correlation exists when a negative error is followed by a positive error, then another negative error, and so on. The error terms alternate between positive and negative values. Positive serial correlation is shown in the right-hand graph. In positive serial correlation, positive errors tend to be followed by other positive errors, while negative errors are followed by other negative errors.

When serial correlation exists, problems can develop in using and interpreting the OLS regression function. The existence of serial correlation does not bias the coefficients that are estimated, but it does make the estimates of the standard errors of b smaller than the true standard errors. This means that the t-ratios calculated for each coefficient will be overstated, which in turn may lead to the rejection of null hypotheses that should not have been rejected. That is, regression coefficients may be deemed statistically significant when indeed they are not. In addition, the existence of serial correlation causes the R^2 and F-statistics

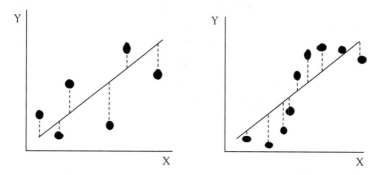

Figure 4.4 Negative (left) and positive serial correlation (right). The residuals (or errors) are indicated by the dashed lines

to be unreliable in evaluating the overall significance of the regression function.[6]

There are ways to test statistically for the existence of serial correlation. The method most frequently used is the evaluation of the Durbin–Watson statistic (DW). This statistic is calculated as follows:

$$DW = \frac{\sum (e_t - e_{t-1})^2}{\sum e_t^2}$$

where e_t is the residual for time period t and e_{t-1} is the residual for the preceding $(t-1)$ time period.[7] The DW statistic will always be in the range of 0 to 4. As the value of the DW statistic approaches 4, the degree of negative serial correlation increases. As the value of the DW statistic approaches 0, positive serial correlation appears more severe. As a rule of thumb, a value close to 2 indicates that there is no serial correlation.

To be more precise in evaluating the significance and meaning of the calculated DW statistic, you must refer to a Durbin–Watson table (see Appendix 4C). In the table, two columns of values labeled d_l (lower bound of DW) and d_u (upper bound of DW) are given for each possible number of independent variables (k, shown along the top of the table). The values in these columns that correspond to the appropriate number of observations (n, shown down the left side of the table) are used in evaluating the calculated value of the DW statistic, using the tests shown in Table 4.2. A specific example using the women's clothing sales model can be found in Appendix 4D.

You might wonder what causes serial correlation. A primary cause of positive serial correlation and the most common form in business/economic analysis is the existence of long-term cycles and trends in the data. Serial correlation can also result from a misspecification of the model. Perhaps the model is misspecified by including too few independent variables or maybe it should be a nonlinear rather than linear model.

If you find a problem with serial correlation you can try several relatively simple things to reduce the problem. One is to use first differences of

---

[6] The F statistic is discussed in Chapter 6.

[7] Appendix 4D describes how to calculate the Durbin–Watson statistic in Excel.

Table 4.2 Evaluating the Durbin–Watson (DW) statistic

Value of the test	Calculated DW	Result
1	$(4 - d_l) < DW < 4$	Negative serial correlation exists
2	$(4 - d_u) < DW < (4 - d_l)$	Result is indeterminate
3	$2 < DW < (4 - d_u)$	No serial correlation exists
4	$d_u < DW < 2$	No serial correlation exists
5	$d_l < DW < d_u$	Result is indeterminate
6	$0 < DW < d_l$	Positive serial correlation exists

the variables rather than the actual values when performing the regression analysis. That is, use the change in each variable from period to period in the regression. Other potential solutions involve adding additional variables and/or nonlinear terms to the model.[8]

The Four-Step Evaluation Procedure: Stoke's Lodge Occupancy Example

In Chapter 1, you were introduced to a time series that represented the number of rooms occupied per month in a large independent hotel—Stoke's Lodge. You are interested in developing and evaluating a regression model that analyzes monthly room occupancy (MRO) at Stoke's Lodge. You think that the average gas price (GP) in dollars per gallon each month may be a good predictor of occupancy. You collect a sample of monthly data from January 2002 to May 2010, which is a total of 101 observations. Table 4.3 shows a shortened section (the first 12 observations) of the data set.

The results of the bivariate regression analysis can be found in Table 4.4. The regression equation is as follows:

$$MRO = 9,322.976 - 1,080.448(GP)$$

---

[8] Chapter 9 includes discussion about incorporating nonlinear terms into an OLS regression model that can sometimes help alleviate a serial correlation problem.

Table 4.3 Monthly data for Stoke's Lodge occupancy and average gas price (the first year only)

Date	Monthly room occupancy (MRO)	Average monthly gas price (GP)
Jan-02	6,575	1.35
Feb-02	7,614	1.46
Mar-02	7,565	1.55
Apr-02	7,940	1.45
May-02	7,713	1.52
Jun-02	9,110	1.81
Jul-02	10,408	1.57
Aug-02	9,862	1.45
Sep-02	9,718	1.60
Oct-02	8,354	1.57
Nov-02	6,442	1.56
Dec-02	6,379	1.46

Table 4.4 Regression results for Stoke's Lodge occupancy simple regression

Regression Statistics				
Multiple R	0.385		DW = 0.691	
R^2	**0.148**			
Adjusted R^2	0.139			
Standard error	1,672.765			
Observations	101			
	Coefficients	Standard error	t Stat	p-Value
Intercept	**9,322.976**	550.151	**16.946**	0.000
GP	**−1,080.448**	260.702	**−4.145**	0.000

Step 1: Evaluate Whether the Stoke's Lodge Model Makes Sense

One would expect there to be an inverse relationship between hotel occupancy and gas price. That is, as gas prices increase, consumers will be less likely to travel and stay in hotels. Therefore, a decrease in hotel occupancy is expected when gas prices rise. The value of the slope on gas price (GP) is indeed negative indicating that as gas price increases, hotel room occupancy (MRO) will decrease. So, the model is logical.

Step 2: Check for Statistical Significance in the Stoke's Lodge Model

You determined that the model makes sense because the slope term is negative. But, is the slope term (statistically) significantly less than zero? Since there is an expected inverse relationship between hotel room occupancy (MRO) and gas price (GP) a one-tailed test as described in Case 2 is appropriate. The null hypothesis is that the slope is greater than or equal to zero (H_0: $\beta \geq 0$). The alternative hypothesis is that the slope is less than zero (H_1: $\beta < 0$). Excel results showed that the standard error of b for this regression is 260.702, so you can calculate the computed test statistic or t-ratio (t_c) as follows:

$$t_c = \frac{b-0}{\text{SE of } b} = \frac{-1080.448-0}{260.702} = -4.145$$

There were 101 observations in the data set, so the number of degrees of freedom is: $df = n - 2 = 101 - 2 = 99$. Then, in the t-table in Appendix 4B, find the row closest to 99 degrees of freedom ($df = 120$) and the column for a one-tailed test with a level of significance of 0.05, and you find the critical value for t to be 1.658. In this case the value of t_c (−4.145) is less (more negative) than the negative critical table value (−1.658). Thus, there is enough statistical evidence to reject the null hypothesis. Therefore, you conclude that there is a statistically significant negative relationship between monthly room occupancy (MRO) and gas price (GP) at the 5 percent level of significance ($\alpha = 0.05$).

Step 3: Determine the Explanatory Power of the Stoke's Lodge Model

For the Stoke's Lodge model presented in Table 4.4 the coefficient of determination is 0.148. This means that 14.8 percent of the variation in monthly room occupancy (the dependent variable) is explained by the model (or by the variation in the independent variable, monthly gas price). This value is relatively low. In Chapters 6 and 8, you will see how this can be improved.

Step 4: Check for Serial Correlation in the Stoke's Lodge Model

As MRO is time-series data, a check for serial correlation is necessary. The DW statistic is calculated to be 0.691. To formally evaluate the DW statistic for the MRO regression you know that $n = 101$ (number of observations) or $k = 1$ (number of independent variables). When the exact numbers for k or n are not provided in the table, use the closest value found in the table. From the DW table in Appendix 4C, you find the lower bound of DW = 1.442 and the upper bound of DW = 1.544. Test 6 in Table 4.2 is satisfied, because the calculated DW statistic of 0.691 is less than the lower bound (1.442) from the DW table. Therefore, positive serial correlation exists in this model. You will see that more complete models may have better results.

Summary and Looking Ahead

In this chapter, you have learned the four-step procedure used to evaluate a simple regression model. First, it is necessary to determine whether the model makes logical sense. If it does not make sense you should not continue with that particular model. Second, you should check for statistical significance of the slope term. It is necessary to determine whether a one or two-tailed test is appropriate based on your expectations about the direction (direct, inverse, or undecided) of the relationship between Y and X. Third, you can determine the explanatory power of the model by evaluating the coefficient of determination or R-square. Finally, if you have time-series data, you need to check for serial correlation or patterns in the residuals. As you read through the rest of the book, you will use this procedure to evaluate simple regression models. Also, in Chapter 6, you will learn to build on your understanding of this four-step procedure in order to evaluate multiple regression models.

What You Have Learned in Chapter 4

- To identify the four-steps involved in evaluating a simple regression model.
- To evaluate whether a simple regression model makes logical sense.
- To check for statistical significance of a slope term.
- To identify when it is appropriate to use a one-tailed versus a two-tailed hypothesis test.
- To evaluate the explanatory power of a simple regression model.
- To check for serial correlation in simple regression models with time-series data.

Appendix 4A: More Details Concerning the Concept of "Degrees of Freedom"

The concept of "degrees of freedom" is fuzzy, to say the least. You might think of this number (df) as the number of values in the calculation of a statistic that are free to vary. The df can be determined by taking the number of individual pieces of information used to calculate a statistic (which in most cases is the total number of observations in your sample, n) minus the number of parameters that you are estimating. That is, each parameter that you are estimating costs you 1 df leaving you with fewer values that are free to vary.

If you have just two points in your regression sample data those two points determine the regression line. Neither can vary without changing the regression equation. In this case, the df would be equal to 0. You start out with two individual pieces of information (two sample data points). In order to estimate the simple regression equation $Y = f(X) = a + bX$ you need to estimate the values of the constant (a) and the slope (b). Each of these will cost you 1 df. If you have more than two data points all of them can vary except for two when you estimate a simple regression equation so the df $= n - 2$.

For multiple regression, df is defined as $n - (k+1)$ where k is the number of independent (X) variables in the model and 1 represents the constant (a). In multiple regression, there are multiple slope terms to estimate and each of these will cost you 1 df.

The important thing for you to know is that when testing a hypothesis df comes into play. For regression df will be $n - 2$ or $n - (k + 1)$. Do you see that for a simple regression with one X variable the two ways to express df are equivalent?

Appendix 4B: Student's *t*-Distribution

df	\multicolumn{4}{c}{Level of significance for one-tailed tests}
	0.10	0.05	0.025	0.01
1	3.078	6.314	12.706	31.821
2	1.886	2.920	4.303	6.965
3	1.638	2.353	3.182	4.541
4	1.533	2.132	2.776	3.747
5	1.476	2.015	2.571	3.365
6	1.440	1.943	2.447	3.143
7	1.415	1.895	2.365	2.998
8	1.397	1.860	2.306	2.896
9	1.383	1.833	2.262	2.821
10	1.372	1.812	2.228	2.764
11	1.363	1.796	2.201	2.718
12	1.356	1.782	2.179	2.681
13	1.350	1.771	2.160	2.650
14	1.345	1.761	2.145	2.624
15	1.341	1.753	2.131	2.602
16	1.337	1.746	2.120	2.583
17	1.333	1.740	2.110	2.567
18	1.330	1.734	2.101	2.552
19	1.328	1.729	2.093	2.539
20	1.325	1.725	2.086	2.528
21	1.323	1.721	2.080	2.518
22	1.321	1.717	2.074	2.508
23	1.319	1.714	2.069	2.500
24	1.318	1.711	2.064	2.492
25	1.316	1.708	2.060	2.485
26	1.315	1.706	2.056	2.479
27	1.314	1.703	2.052	2.473
28	1.313	1.701	2.048	2.467
29	1.311	1.699	2.045	2.462
30	1.310	1.697	2.042	2.457
40	1.303	1.684	2.021	2.423
60	1.296	1.671	2.000	2.390
120	1.289	1.658	1.980	2.358
∞	1.282	1.645	1.960	2.326
	0.20	0.10	0.05	0.02
	\multicolumn{4}{c}{Level of significance for two-tailed tests}

Source: Modified from, NIST/SEMATECH e-Handbook of Statistical Methods, www.itl.nist. gov/ div898/handbook/, February 6, 2012.

Appendix 4C: Critical Values for the Lower and Upper Bounds on the Distribution of the Durbin–Watson Statistic*

Five Percent Level

n	k=1 d_L	k=1 d_U	k=2 d_L	k=2 d_U	k=3 d_L	k=3 d_U	k=4 d_L	k=4 d_U	k=5 d_L	k=5 d_U	k=6 d_L	k=6 d_U	k=7 d_L	k=7 d_U	k=8 d_L	k=8 d_U	k=9 d_L	k=9 d_U	k=10 d_L	k=10 d_U
6	0.610	1.400	---	---	---	---	---	---	---	---	---	---	---	---	---	---	---	---	---	---
7	0.700	1.356	0.467	1.896	---	---	---	---	---	---	---	---	---	---	---	---	---	---	---	---
8	0.763	1.332	0.559	1.777	0.368	2.287	---	---	---	---	---	---	---	---	---	---	---	---	---	---
9	0.824	1.320	0.629	1.699	0.455	2.128	0.296	2.588	---	---	---	---	---	---	---	---	---	---	---	---
10	0.879	1.320	0.697	1.641	0.525	2.016	0.376	2.414	0.243	2.822	---	---	---	---	---	---	---	---	---	---
11	0.927	1.324	0.758	1.604	0.595	1.928	0.444	2.283	0.316	2.645	0.203	3.005	---	---	---	---	---	---	---	---
12	0.971	1.331	0.812	1.579	0.658	1.864	0.512	2.177	0.379	2.506	0.268	2.832	0.171	3.149	---	---	---	---	---	---
13	1.010	1.340	0.861	1.562	0.715	1.816	0.574	2.094	0.445	2.390	0.328	2.692	0.230	2.985	0.147	3.266	---	---	---	---
14	1.045	1.350	0.905	1.551	0.767	1.779	0.632	2.030	0.505	2.296	0.389	2.572	0.286	2.848	0.200	3.111	0.127	3.360	---	---
15	1.077	1.361	0.946	1.543	0.814	1.750	0.685	1.977	0.562	2.220	0.447	2.472	0.343	2.727	0.251	2.979	0.175	3.216	0.111	3.438
16	1.106	1.371	0.982	1.539	0.857	1.728	0.734	1.935	0.615	2.157	0.502	2.388	0.398	2.624	0.304	2.860	0.222	3.090	0.155	3.304
17	1.133	1.381	1.015	1.536	0.897	1.710	0.779	1.900	0.664	2.104	0.554	2.318	0.451	2.537	0.356	2.757	0.272	2.975	0.198	3.184
18	1.158	1.391	1.046	1.535	0.933	1.696	0.820	1.872	0.710	2.060	0.603	2.257	0.502	2.461	0.407	2.667	0.321	2.873	0.244	3.073
19	1.180	1.401	1.074	1.536	0.967	1.685	0.859	1.848	0.752	2.023	0.649	2.206	0.549	2.396	0.456	2.589	0.369	2.783	0.290	2.974
20	1.201	1.411	1.100	1.537	0.998	1.676	0.894	1.828	0.792	1.991	0.692	2.162	0.595	2.339	0.502	2.521	0.416	2.704	0.336	2.885
21	1.221	1.420	1.125	1.538	1.026	1.669	0.927	1.812	0.829	1.964	0.732	2.124	0.637	2.290	0.547	2.460	0.461	2.633	0.380	2.806
22	1.239	1.429	1.147	1.541	1.053	1.664	0.958	1.797	0.863	1.940	0.769	2.090	0.677	2.246	0.588	2.407	0.504	2.571	0.424	2.734

n																				
23	1.257	1.437	1.168	1.543	1.078	1.660	0.986	1.785	0.895	1.920	0.804	2.061	0.715	2.208	0.628	2.360	0.545	2.514	0.465	2.670
24	1.273	1.446	1.188	1.546	1.101	1.656	1.013	1.775	0.925	1.902	0.837	2.035	0.751	2.174	0.666	2.318	0.584	2.464	0.506	2.613
25	1.288	1.454	1.206	1.550	1.123	1.654	1.038	1.767	0.953	1.886	0.868	2.012	0.784	2.144	0.702	2.280	0.621	2.419	0.544	2.560
26	1.302	1.461	1.224	1.553	1.143	1.652	1.062	1.759	0.979	1.873	0.897	1.992	0.816	2.117	0.735	2.246	0.657	2.379	0.581	2.513
27	1.316	1.469	1.240	1.556	1.162	1.651	1.084	1.753	1.004	1.861	0.925	1.974	0.845	2.093	0.767	2.216	0.691	2.342	0.616	2.470
28	1.328	1.476	1.255	1.560	1.181	1.650	1.104	1.747	1.028	1.850	0.951	1.958	0.874	2.071	0.798	2.188	0.723	2.309	0.650	2.431
29	1.341	1.483	1.270	1.563	1.198	1.650	1.124	1.743	1.050	1.841	0.975	1.944	0.900	2.052	0.826	2.164	0.753	2.278	0.682	2.396
30	1.352	1.489	1.284	1.567	1.214	1.650	1.143	1.739	1.071	1.833	0.998	1.931	0.926	2.034	0.854	2.141	0.782	2.251	0.712	2.363
31	1.363	1.496	1.297	1.570	1.229	1.650	1.160	1.735	1.090	1.825	1.020	1.920	0.950	2.018	0.879	2.120	0.810	2.226	0.741	2.333
32	1.373	1.502	1.309	1.574	1.244	1.650	1.177	1.732	1.109	1.819	1.041	1.909	0.972	2.004	0.904	2.102	0.836	2.203	0.769	2.306
33	1.383	1.508	1.321	1.577	1.258	1.651	1.193	1.730	1.127	1.813	1.061	1.900	0.994	1.991	0.927	2.085	0.861	2.181	0.795	2.281
34	1.393	1.514	1.333	1.580	1.271	1.652	1.208	1.728	1.144	1.808	1.080	1.891	1.015	1.979	0.950	2.069	0.885	2.162	0.821	2.257
35	1.402	1.519	1.343	1.584	1.283	1.653	1.222	1.726	1.160	1.803	1.097	1.884	1.034	1.967	0.971	2.054	0.908	2.144	0.845	2.236
36	1.411	1.525	1.354	1.587	1.295	1.654	1.236	1.724	1.175	1.799	1.114	1.877	1.053	1.957	0.991	2.041	0.930	2.127	0.868	2.216
37	1.419	1.530	1.364	1.590	1.307	1.655	1.249	1.723	1.190	1.795	1.131	1.870	1.071	1.948	1.011	2.029	0.951	2.112	0.891	2.198
38	1.427	1.535	1.373	1.594	1.318	1.656	1.261	1.722	1.204	1.792	1.146	1.864	1.088	1.939	1.029	2.017	0.970	2.098	0.912	2.180
39	1.435	1.540	1.382	1.597	1.328	1.658	1.273	1.722	1.218	1.789	1.161	1.859	1.104	1.932	1.047	2.007	0.990	2.085	0.932	2.164
40	1.442	1.544	1.391	1.600	1.338	1.659	1.285	1.721	1.230	1.786	1.175	1.854	1.120	1.924	1.064	1.997	1.008	2.072	0.945	2.149

*k is the number of independent variables in the equation excluding the constant; n is the number of observations.

Source: N.E. Savin, and K.E. White, "The Durbin–Watson Test for Serial Correlation with Extreme Sample Sizes or Many Regressions," (Tables II and III), *Econometrica* vol. 45, 1977, pp. 1989–1996. Used with permission of *Econometrica*.

Appendix 4D: Calculating the Durbin–Watson Statistic in Excel

As you have learned in this chapter, the DW statistic is often used to evaluate the existence of serial correlation. Remember that serial correlation refers to patterns in the error terms (or residuals, e) over time. The formula for this calculation is:

$$DW = \frac{\sum (e_t - e_{t-1})^2}{\sum e_t^{\,2}}$$

To illustrate how you can calculate the DW statistic in Excel, consider the linear regression trend for annual women's clothing sales (AWCS) data introduced in Chapter 3. The regression trend equation was:

$$AWCS = 30{,}709.200 + 773.982(\text{Year}).$$

The graph is reproduced as Figure 4D.1 and the calculation of DW statistic in Excel is shown in Table 4D.1.

When using Excel for regression with time-series data you want to check the box for "residuals." Residual is another name for error (e). Errors are calculated as the actual values minus the predicted values (based on the regression line). From that "residuals" column it is easy to use Excel to calculate the DW statistic. This is shown in Table 4D.1 (parts added to the Excel output are in **bold**).

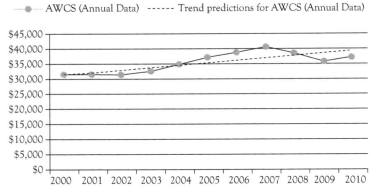

Figure 4D.1 Actual AWCS and the trend regression result. Here you see in a graph how some negative errors are followed by a set of positive errors then more negative errors

Table 4D.1 The calculation of DW statistic from Excel regression output. Note the pattern in the signs for the errors

Residual output				
Observation/ year	Predicted AWCS (annual data)	Residuals = e_t	$(e_t - e_{t-1})^2$	$(e_t)^2$
1	31,483	−3.2	NA	10.124
2	32,257	−770	588,261	593,152
3	33,031	−1,751	962,325	3,066,510
4	33,805	−1,207	295,956	1,457,156
5	34,579	307	2,292,251	94,182
6	35,353	1,647	1,795,649	2,712,310
7	36,127	2,589	887,398	6,702,544
8	36,901	3,436	717,440	11,805,721
9	37,675	676	7,617,500	456,927
10	38,449	−2,669	11,188,903	7,123,658
11	39,223	−2,254	172,240	5,080,516
		Sums =	26,517,923	39,092,687
		DW =	0.678	

Remember that the ideal value for DW statistic is 2.0. Values between 2.0 and 4.0 suggest possible negative serial correlation, whereas values between 0.0 and 2.0 suggest possible positive serial correlation.

If you look at the graph of the regression results (Figure 4D.1) you can see that there are four negative errors, then five positive errors, and finally two more negative errors. This can also be seen in Table 4D.1, where you also see that the calculated value for DW = 0.678. This clearly represents positive serial correlation.

To formally evaluate the DW statistic for the AWCS regression trend you know that $n = 11$ (number of observations) and $k = 1$ (number of independent variables). From the DW table in Appendix 4C you find the lower bound of DW = 0.927 and the upper bound of DW = 1.324. Test 6 (see the table on the following page) is satisfied, so you know this model has positive serial correlation. You see that the calculated DW statistic of 0.678 is less than the lower bound (0.927) from the DW table.

Value of the test	Calculated DW	Result
1	$(4 - d_l) < DW < 4$	Negative serial correlation exists
2	$(4 - d_u) < DW < (4 - d_l)$	Result is indeterminate
3	$2 < DW < (4 - d_u)$	No serial correlation exists
4	$d_u < DW < 2$	No serial correlation exists
5	$d_l < DW < d_u$	Result is indeterminate
6	$0 < DW < d_l$	Positive serial correlation exists

CHAPTER 5

Point and Interval Estimates From a Regression Model

Chapter 5 Preview

When you have completed reading this chapter you will be able to:

- Learn to calculate a point estimate based on a regression equation.
- Understand that this point estimate is the best estimate based on regression statistics.
- Learn to calculate an approximate 95 percent confidence interval centered on the point estimate.
- Realize that regression with one independent (or causal) variable is quite limited for business applications.
- See that larger models with more causal variables can increase the explanatory power of regression.
- See that larger models with more causal variables can result in more narrow (more precise) approximate 95 percent confidence intervals centered on the point estimate.

Introduction

In Chapter 3, you saw simple bivariate regression equations for women's clothing sales and for college basketball team's WP. In this chapter, you will learn to apply these two models. You will use both to a make point estimate and an approximate 95 percent confidence interval centered on the point estimate for the dependent variables.

The Concept of a Point Estimate

A point estimate is a single value, or point. It is your best estimate (or prediction) of the value of a dependent variable, given some value(s) for the independent variables(s). The point estimate is generated directly from the regression equation. To illustrate, suppose that you have a very simple regression model as follows:

$$SALES = f(PER\ CAPITA\ INCOME)$$
$$SALES = -10 + 0.002(PER\ CAPITA\ INCOME)$$

If per capita income is \$30,000 then your point estimate (or prediction) of sales would be:

$$SALES = -10 + (0.002 \times 30,000) = -10 + 60 = 50$$

While this would be your best estimate it is likely to be wrong. This may sound disturbing to you. However, statistical theory supports the notion that this best estimate will be close to correct most of the time. It just may not be exactly right. Suppose in this example sales are in thousands of units. Your estimate of sales is really 50,000 units … not 50,001 or 49,999 but exactly 50,000. The business world is not so precise. If sales really turn out to be 50,001 and you estimated sales to be 50,000 you would look pretty good. But technically you would be wrong. Later in this chapter, you will see how to calculate point estimates for some of the models you have seen in previous chapters.

The Concept of Approximate
95 Percent Confidence Interval Estimates

Because you would almost always be wrong (but close) with a point estimate you may want to provide a set of lower and upper bounds for an estimate such that you would have some level of confidence that the true value would be in that interval. To do this you need to know another statistic called the "standard error" of the estimate (SEE). The SEE is just called standard error in Excel.[1] This measure is included in the output of almost every regression software program.[2]

The approximate 95 percent confidence interval is found by taking your point estimate plus and minus two times the standard error of the estimate (SEE) as follows:

Point Estimate ± 2(Standard Error of the Estimate)

The number 2 in this calculation is an approximation for 1.96 from the t-table with a large number of degrees of freedom. This confidence interval is also an approximation because the true confidence interval bows away from the regression line as the dependent variable and the independent variable(s) move away from their respective mean values.

---

[1] The standard error of the estimate may also be represented by SER or SEE (standard error of the regression or standard error of the estimate, respectively). In Excel, it is simply called the standard error and is found near the top of regression results in the section headed "*Regression Statistics.*"

[2] However, it can be calculated as follows: SEE = $[(\sum (Y_i - Y_{iE})^2 \div (n - 2)]^{0.5}$ where n is the number of observations used in the estimation of the regression equation (the 0.5 power is the same as the square root).

You will see this concept applied later in this chapter for regression models you have already seen. After seeing some examples of the concept you should find it easy to apply in your own situation.

There is a way to get an exact 95 percent confidence interval. The arithmetic is a bit more complex but it can be done.[3] However, relying on the approximate 95 percent confidence interval is sufficient for most purposes.[4]

Point Estimates in Practice: Two Examples

Women's Clothing Sales

Consider the following women's clothing sales (WCS) model first introduced in Chapter 2. In this model WCS was a function of personal income (PI). The model was:

$$WCS = 1,187.123 + 0.165(PI)$$

---

[3] While an approximation for a 95 percent confidence interval is often used because of its simplicity, a more precise interval estimation procedure is available:
$$Y = Y_E \pm [t(SE)[1 + (1/n) + (X_o - X_M)^2 / \Sigma (X_i - X_M)^2]]$$
where
Y_E = point estimate from the regression equation
SE = standard error or standard error of the *estimate* (SEE) or standard error of the *regression* (SER)
t = t-table value at the desired two-tailed significance level and n–2 degrees of freedom
n = number of observations used in estimating the regression model
X_o = value of the independent variable for which the estimate of Y is desired
X_M = mean value of the independent variable
$\Sigma (X_i - X_M)^2$ = the squared deviations of the independent variable from its mean value for all n observations
In this formulation for the confidence interval, you can see that the width of the interval depends on the value of the independent variable for which the estimation is made (i.e., on the value of X_o). Also, note that the interval becomes wider the farther X_o is from X_M.

[4] Statisticians will sometimes make a distinction between a confidence interval and a prediction interval. For practical understanding of regression this distinction is not important to you. For example, in *Applied Statistical Methods* (Carlson and Thorne, Prentice-Hall, 1997, p. 664) the terms are used interchangeably.

In Chapter 2, you put a value for personal income into this equation to get an estimate of WCS for that level of personal income. This was a point estimate because you obtained a single number for your answer. In that example, you estimated the dollar amount of WCS if personal income is 9,000 (billion dollars). You obtained:

$$WCS = 1{,}187.123 + (0.165 \times 9{,}000)$$
$$WCS = 1{,}187.123 + 1{,}485 = 2{,}672.123$$

Thus, your estimate of WCS if personal income was 9,000 (billion dollars) is 2,672.123 (million dollars) or \$2,672,123,000. Do you think this would be exactly right for that level of PI? Probably not!

Winning Percentage for College Basketball Teams

In the second example, consider the model for the WP of college basketball teams, also shown in Chapter 2. The model was:

$$WP = -198.9 + 5.707(FG)$$

In Chapter 2, you learned that if a team's FG percentage is 45 percent your best estimate of the team's WP would be:

$$WP = -198.9 + 5.707(FG)$$
$$WP = -198.9 + (5.707 \times 45) = 57.9$$

This probably seems awfully precise to you. Would you be sure the WP might not be 57.6 percent or maybe 58.1 percent? Again, probably not. But 57.9 percent would be your best point estimate (prediction) of a team's conference winning percentage (WP) when a team's FG percentage is 45 percent. If you need to provide one number as your estimate, 59.7 percent would be the best number to give.

Approximate 95 Percent Confidence Interval Estimates: Two Examples

While point estimates are useful, it is very unlikely that they will be exactly correct. Thus, it is often preferable to make an interval estimate in such a way that you can be 95 percent confident that the true value will be somewhere within the interval. You have seen that an approximation for a 95 percent confidence interval can be given as:

$$\text{Point Estimate} \pm 2(\text{SEE})$$

where SEE is the standard error of the estimate.[5]

Before looking at examples, you should know exactly where to find the SEE in Excel's regression output. Look at the partial output from an Excel regression in Table 5.1. You see that the SEE is in the top section of Excel's output under the heading "Regression Statistics." In this example, the SEE is 1.676. To calculate an approximate 95 percent confidence interval for this model you would have:

$$\text{Point Estimate} \pm 2(\text{SEE})$$
$$\text{Point Estimate} \pm 2(1.676)$$

You would need the entire regression equation to get your point estimate. For now the important thing is for you to know where to find the SEE in your regression results from Excel. In the examples that follow you will see how to do specific calculations.

Table 5.1 Partial regression results from Excel for a market share model. The standard error (SE) is in bold and a slightly larger type. This model will be discussed fully in Chapter 7

Summary output	
Regression Statistics	
Multiple R	0.929
R-square	0.863
Adjusted R-square	0.812
Standard error	**1.676**
Observations	12

---

[5] Remember that the standard error (SE) can also be referred to as the standard error of the estimate (SEE) or the standard error of the regression (SER) depending on the software you use. In Excel it is "standard error."

Women's Clothing Sales: Example One

As you have seen, the relationship between women's clothing sales (WCS) and personal income (PI) is:

$$WCS = 1{,}187.123 + 0.165(PI)$$

Next, let's assume that for PI = 9,000

$$WCS = 1{,}187.123 + (0.165 \times 9{,}000)$$
$$WCS = 1{,}187.123 + 1{,}485 = 2{,}672.123$$

This is the point estimate (prediction). Table 5.2 provides the Excel output needed to get the approximate 95 percent confidence interval. Here you see that the SEE is 525.160. You now have enough information to calculate the approximate 95 percent confidence interval. The point estimate of 2,672.123 is your starting point and the SEE is 525.160. The approximate 95 percent confidence interval is:

$$\text{Point Estimate} \pm 2(SEE)$$
$$2{,}672.123 \pm 2(SEE)$$
$$2{,}672.123 \pm 2(525.160)$$

Table 5.2 *Partial Excel output for women's clothing sales as a function of personal income. The ANOVA part of the output is omitted here*

Summary output				
Regression Statistics				
Multiple R	0.416			
R-square	0.173			
Adjusted R-square	0.167			
Standard error	**525.160**			
Observations	135			
	Coefficients	**Standard error**	**t Stat**	**p-Value**
Intercept	1,187.123	335.390	3.540	0.001
PI	0.165	0.031	5.277	0.000

$$2{,}672.123 \pm 1{,}050.320$$
$$1{,}621.803 \text{ to } 3{,}722.443$$

This is based on how WCS are influenced by only a single independent variable, personal income. As shown in Table 5.2, the coefficient of determination (R^2) is 0.173. Thus, this simple model only explains about 17.3 percent of the variation in WCS.

As you would expect WCS are influenced by more than just PI. As you learn more about regression you will see how you can include many other measures that may influence WCS into a regression model. If, in addition to personal income, you include the unemployment rate among women, an index of consumer sentiment, and measures to account for seasonality you can develop a much better regression model. If we include them the coefficient of determination increases to 0.966.[6] This means that the more complete model explains 96.6 percent of the variation in WCS. Partial regression statistics for this model is shown in Table 5.3.

With the more complete model the approximate 95 percent confidence interval becomes narrower as follows:

Point Estimate $\pm$ 2(SEE)
Point Estimate $\pm$ 2(105.403)
Point Estimate $\pm$ 210.806

Table 5.3 Partial regression statistics for a more complete model of women's clothing sales. The SEE is much smaller than the SEE in Table 5.2

Summary output	
Regression Statistics	
Multiple R	0.985
R-square	0.970
Adjusted R-square	0.966
Standard error	105.403
Observations	135

[6] When you use multiple independent variables you use the adjusted R^2 for the coefficient of determination.

Table 5.4 Comparison of two models for basketball winning percentage

Regression Statistics		Regression Statistics	
Multiple R	0.632	Multiple R	0.924
R-square	0.399	R-square	0.853
Adjusted R-square	0.391	Adjusted R-square	0.828
Standard error	16.472	Standard error	8.760
Observations	82	Observations	82
Small bivariate regression model		Larger regression model	

Compare this plus or minus range (210.806) with the one for the simpler models (1,050.320).

You see that by including more causal variables two important things change. The coefficient of determination increases from 16.7 percent to 96.6 percent, and the standard error decreases from 525.160 to 105.403. As a result, the width of the approximate 95 percent confidence interval falls from 1,050.320 to 210.806. This allows you to be more precise in your estimates based on a regression model.

Basketball Winning Percentage Example

Statistics play an important role in sports, as illustrated by the book and the movie *MONEYBALL*, which was based on a true story. You have already seen one model of the collegiate basketball WP in which only the percentage of successful FG attempts was used as a causal variable. That model explained about 40 percent of the variation in WP. If you were to include other offensive and some defensive measures you could develop a model that would explain roughly 83 percent of the variation in WP.

The regression statistics for both of these models are shown in Table 5.4. You see that in the larger regression model the explanatory power is about twice as high as with the smaller model and the SEE is much smaller.

For these two models, the widths of the approximate 95 percent confidence bands would be:

Small Model: Point Estimate $\pm$ 2(16.472) = Point Estimate $\pm$ 32.944
Larger Model: Point Estimate $\pm$ 2(8.760) = Point Estimate $\pm$ 17.520

Again you see that the width of the approximate 95 percent confidence band depends on the model. Rarely is a model with only one independent variable sufficient in business applications. Beginning in Chapter 6 you will build on what you have learned about the basics of regression analysis to build larger, more complex, and more useful regression models.

What You Have Learned in Chapter 5

- You can calculate a point estimate based on a regression equation.
- You know that a point estimate is the best estimate based on regression statistics.
- You can calculate an approximate 95 percent confidence interval centered on the point estimate.
- You realize that regression with one independent (or causal) variable is quite limited for business applications.
- You have seen that larger models with more causal variables can increase the explanatory power of regression.
- You have seen that larger models with more causal variables can result in more narrow (more precise) approximate 95 percent confidence intervals centered on the point estimate.

CHAPTER 6

Multiple Linear Regression

Chapter 6 Preview

When you have completed reading this chapter you will be able to:

- Identify the five steps involved in evaluating a multiple regression model.
- Evaluate whether a multiple regression model makes logical sense.
- Check for statistical significance of all slope terms in a multiple regression model.
- Use the p-value method to evaluate statistical significance.
- Evaluate the explanatory power of a multiple regression model.
- Test the overall significance of a multiple regression model.
- Check for serial correlation in multiple regression models with time-series data.
- Check for multicollinearity in multiple regression models.
- Make point and interval estimates based on a multiple regression model.

Introduction

At this point, you are familiar with the basics of ordinary least squares (OLS) simple regression analysis where you use one independent variable to explain variation in the dependent variable. You know how to run simple regression in Excel, evaluate simple regression models using the four-step procedure, and make point or interval estimates of the dependent variable in a simple regression model based on some given value of the independent variable. In this chapter, you will learn how to expand simple regression models to include multiple independent variables. When performing multiple regression analysis there are some modifications and additions needed to the four-step evaluation procedure discussed previously for simple regression.

Multiple Linear Regression

In many (perhaps most) applications, the dependent variable of interest is a function of more than one independent variable. That is, there is more than one independent variable that can be used to explain variation in the dependent variable. In such cases, a form of OLS regression called multiple linear regression is appropriate. This is a straightforward extension of simple linear regression and is built upon the same basic set of assumptions. The general form of the multiple linear regression model is:

$$Y = f(X_1, X_2, ..., X_k)$$

and the regression equation becomes:

$$Y = a + b_1 X_1 + b_2 X_2 + ... + b_k X_k$$

where Y represents the dependent variable and X_i represent each of the k different independent variables. The intercept, or constant, term in the regression is a and the b_i terms represent the slope, or rate of change, associated with each of the k independent variables in the model.

The addition of more independent variables to the basic regression model is almost always helpful in developing better models of economic and business relationships. Doing so, however, does mean a bit of modification to the four-step evaluation process used to evaluate simple regression models with only one independent variable (discussed in Chapter 4). You will recall that those four steps involved answering these questions:

1. Does the model make sense? That is, is it consistent with a logical view of the situation being investigated?

2. Is there a statistically significant relationship between the dependent and independent variables?

3. What percentage of the variation in the dependent variable does the regression model explain?

4. Is there a problem of serial correlation among the error terms in the model?

For multiple regression analysis, you need to add a fifth question:

5. Is there multicollinearity among the independent variables? Multicollinearity occurs when two or more of the independent variables in multiple regression are highly correlated with each other.

Let us now consider each of these five questions and how they can be answered for a specific multiple regression model.

Stoke's Lodge Multiple Linear Regression Example

Reconsider the simple regression analysis that you were introduced to in Chapter 4 on monthly room occupancy (MRO) at Stoke's Lodge. Average gas price (GP) in dollars per gallon per month was the only independent variable in the model and you obtained the following regression equation:

$$MRO = 9,322.976 - 1,080.448(GP)$$

However, you know that during the time period being considered there was a considerable expansion in the number of casinos in the State where Stoke's Lodge is located, most of which have integrated lodging facilities available. So, you decide to collect monthly data from January 2002 to May 2010 on the number of casino employees (CEs) working in the State (in thousands) because you want to include this as an additional independent variable in your regression model. Table 6.1 shows a shortened section (the first 24 observations) of the data set.

The results of the multiple regression analysis can be found in Table 6.2. The regression equation is as follows:

$$MRO = 15,484.483 - 1,097.686(GP) - 1,013.646(CE)$$

Table 6.1 *Monthly data for Stoke's Lodge occupancy, average gas price, and number of casino employees (the first two years only)*

Date	Monthly room occupancy (MRO)	Average monthly gas price (GP)	Monthly casino employees in thousands (CE)
Jan-02	6,575	1.35	5.3
Feb-02	7,614	1.46	5.2
Mar-02	7,565	1.55	5.2
Apr-02	7,940	1.45	5.2
May-02	7,713	1.52	5.1
Jun-02	9,110	1.81	5.0
Jul-02	10,408	1.57	5.0
Aug-02	9,862	1.45	5.0
Sep-02	9,718	1.60	5.1
Oct-02	8,354	1.57	5.8
Nov-02	6,442	1.56	6.6
Dec-02	6,379	1.46	6.4
Jan-03	5,585	1.51	6.4
Feb-03	6,032	1.49	6.4
Mar-03	8,739	1.43	6.3
Apr-03	7,628	1.62	6.3
May-03	9,234	1.83	6.3
Jun-03	11,144	1.63	6.3
Jul-03	8,986	1.36	6.2
Aug-03	10,303	1.52	6.2
Sep-03	8,480	1.67	6.2
Oct-03	9,135	1.28	6.2
Nov-03	6,793	1.17	6.2
Dec-03	5,735	1.13	6.4

Notice that there is a slope term associated with gas price (−1,097.686) and another slope term associated with casino employees (−1,013.646). Let's evaluate this model!

Evaluation Step 1: Evaluate Whether the Model Makes Sense

First and foremost, your regression model still must be logical. There is nothing different about this step of the evaluation procedure except for

Table 6.2 Regression results for Stoke's Lodge occupancy multiple regression

Regression Statistics					
Multiple R	0.466		DW = 0.7303		
R-square	0.217				
Adjusted R-square	0.201				
Standard error	1,611.772				
Observations	101				
ANOVA					
	df	SS	MS	F	*Sig F*
Regression	2	70,491,333	35,245,666.7	13.567	0.000
Residual	98	254,585,374	2,597,809.94		
Total	100	325,076,708			
	Coefficients	Standard error	*t* Stat	*p*-value	*p/2*
Intercept	15,484.483	2,162.820	7.159	0.000	0.000
GP	−1,097.686	251.265	−4.369	0.000	0.000
CE	−1,013.646	344.959	−2.938	0.004	0.002

the fact that you have multiple independent variables and therefore you must evaluate the sign of *each* of the slope terms in the model to make sure that they each make logical sense.

For the Stoke's Lodge multiple regression model, a negative slope is still expected for gas price because higher gas prices will deter people from traveling and therefore room occupancy is expected to decline. But, what about the slope term on casino employees? The idea here is that the expansion of the casino industry has caused a decline in the occupancy at Stoke's Lodge because these new casinos have integrated lodging facilities and are considered to be competitive. Therefore, a negative slope is also expected for casino employees because more employees working in the casino industry indicates an increase in competition and should result in a decline in occupancy at Stoke's Lodge. The OLS equation was found to be:

$$MRO = 15,484.483 - 1,097.686(GP) - 1,013.646(CE)$$

We see that the signs on both GP and CE are indeed negative and so this model does make logical sense.

Evaluation Step 2: Check for Statistical Significance

Similar to step 1, there is little difference in this step of the evaluation procedure except for the fact that you have multiple independent variables and therefore you must check for the statistical significance of *each* of the slope terms in the model. Therefore, you will have multiple hypotheses to test. However, it should be noted that the degrees of freedom (df) is different between simple and multiple linear regression. In multiple regression, the appropriate number of degrees of freedom (df) is: $df = n - (k + 1)$, where n equals the number of observations used in your sample and k is the number of independent variables used in the model.

Recall from Chapter 4 that the statistical test of significance of a regression slope (b_i) can take any of the following three forms depending on the relationship that you are analyzing:

Case 1: This form is appropriate when you are testing for the existence of any linear functional relationship between Y and X.

$$H_0 : \beta = 0$$
$$H_1 : \beta \neq 0$$

Case 2: This form is appropriate if you think that the relationship between Y and X is an inverse (negative) one.

$$H_0 : \beta \geq 0$$
$$H_1 : \beta < 0$$

Case 3: This form is appropriate if you think that the relationship between Y and X is a direct (positive) one.

$$H_0 : \beta \leq 0$$
$$H_1 : \beta > 0$$

For the Stoke's Lodge example, the model makes sense because the slope term on both gas price (GP) and casino employees (CE) was negative. But, are these slope terms significantly less than zero? Since there is an expected inverse relationship between monthly hotel room occupancy (MRO) and gas price (GP) a one-tailed test as described in Case 2 is appropriate. Similarly, since there is an expected inverse relationship between monthly hotel room occupancy (MRO) and casino employees (CE) a one-tailed test as described in Case 2 is appropriate for this independent variable as well.

First, let's test for significance of the slope term on gas price (GP). The null hypothesis is that the slope is greater than or equal to zero (H_0: $\beta \geq 0$). The alternative hypothesis is that the slope is less than zero (H_1: $\beta < 0$). Excel results showed that the standard error for the slope on GP is 251.265, so you can calculate the computed test statistic (or t-ratio), t_c, for GP as follows:

$$t_c = \frac{b - 0}{\text{SE of } b} = \frac{-1,097.686 - 0}{251.265} = -4.369$$

There were 101 observations in the data set and two independent variables in the model, so df $= n - (k + 1) = 101 - (2 + 1) = 98$. Looking at the t-table in Appendix 4B, find the row for 98 df and the column for a one-tailed test with a level of significance of 0.05, and you get the critical value from the t-table to be 1.658.[1] Thus, in this case the absolute value of the computed test statistic (t_c) for GP ($|-4.369|$) is greater than the critical t-table value (1.658) and you have enough statistical evidence to reject the null hypothesis. Therefore, you conclude that there is a statistically significant negative relationship between MRO and GP at the 5 percent level of significance ($\alpha = 0.05$).

Next, let's test for significance of the slope term for casino employees (CE). The null hypothesis is that the slope is greater than or equal to zero (H_0: $\beta \geq 0$). The alternative hypothesis is that the slope is less than zero

---

[1] The t-table in Appendix 4B does not provide critical values for 98 df. Therefore, you can approximate it with the value for 120 df, the closest value in the table.

$(H_1 : \beta < 0)$. Excel results showed that the standard error for the slope on CE is 344.959, so you can calculate the computed test statistic (t_c) for CE as follows:

$$t_c = \frac{b - 0}{\text{SE of } b} = \frac{-1013.646 - 0}{344.959} = -2.938$$

Again, there were 101 observations in the data set and two independent variables in the model, so df $= n - (k + 1) = 101 - (2 + 1) = 98$. It is a one-tailed test and the level of significance is still 0.05 so the critical t-table value is still the same as found above for the hypothesis test on gas price. Thus, in this case the absolute value of t_c for CE ($|-2.938|$) is greater than the critical t-table value (1.658) and you have enough statistical evidence to reject the null hypothesis. Therefore, you conclude that there is a statistically significant negative relationship between MRO and CE at the 5 percent level of significance ($\alpha = 0.05$). That is, gas price (GP) and casino employees (CE) are both considered statistically significant in their negative relationship with occupancy (MRO) at the 95 percent confidence level.

P-Values: A Short-Cut to Determining Statistical Significance

You may have noticed that there is a column in the Excel regression computer output next to the t-stat that is labeled "p-value." The p-value can be used as a quick way to evaluate statistical significance and can be used as an alternative to comparing the computed test statistic, t_c, with the critical t-table value(s). It applies to either simple or multiple regression analysis.

The p-value is the probability of observing another computed test statistic or t-stat that is more extreme (either positive or negative) than the one computed for your sample. Therefore, the smaller the p-value, the more support for the alternative hypothesis. That is, a small p-value implies a small chance of ever obtaining another sample with a slope term more statistically different from zero than the slope term is for your sample.

Consider the p-value for casino employees (CE) which is 0.004. This means that there is a 0.4 percent probability of observing another computed t-stat that is more extreme than the one computed for this sample

($t_c = -2.938$). This probability is illustrated by the shaded regions of the graph in Figure 6.1.

The shaded regions in Figure 6.1 would be relevant if you were performing a two-tailed test (Case 1) and just concerned about whether the slope of CE was statistically *different* (either higher or lower) from zero. However, because you are performing a left-tailed test (Case 2) for the slope on CE and only concerned about whether the slope is statistically *less* than zero you must divide the *p*-value by 2 because only the probability in the left tail of the distribution is relevant. Similarly, when performing a right-tailed test (Case 3) you must divide the *p*-value by 2 because only the probability in the right tail of the distribution is relevant as you are testing whether the slope is statistically *greater* than zero. In Table 6.2, a column is created next to the *p*-value labeled "*p*/2" that can be used when evaluating significance for one-tailed tests (Case 2 or Case 3).

So, you may be wondering how the *p*-value (two-tailed test) or *p*-value/2 (one-tailed test) helps you to determine statistical significance. A simple comparison is made with the level of significance. For situations such as that described in Case 1, the null hypothesis is rejected and

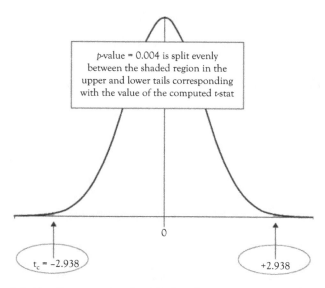

Figure 6.1 P-value associated with the slope on casino employees (CE) in the Stoke's Lodge multiple regression example

you conclude that the true slope is different from zero if the p-value is less than or equal to the desired level of significance, α. For situations such as that described in Case 2, the null hypothesis is rejected and you conclude that the true slope is less than zero if the p-value/2 is less than or equal to the level of significance, α. Finally, for situations such as that described in Case 3, the null hypothesis is rejected and you conclude that the true slope is greater than zero if the p-value/2 is less than or equal to the level of significance, α. This assumes that you have already passed evaluation step one, so you have a logical model. Again, if you do not satisfy evaluation step one nothing else matters.

Now, back to the Stoke's Lodge multiple regression example where you expected both the slope on gas price (GP) and the slope on casino employees (CE) to be negative and therefore needed to perform left-tailed tests to determine statistical significance. As a result, p-value/2 is the relevant statistic in each case and can be found in the Excel regression output in Table 6.2. The p-value/2 is 0.000 for GP and 0.002 for CE. Since both values are less than the level of significance ($\alpha = 0.05$), the null hypothesis is rejected in both instances and both the slope for GP and CE are statistically less than zero (significant), at a 95 percent confidence level. Again, this indicates statistically significant inverse relationships between both independent variables (GP and CE) and the dependent variable (MRO).

Evaluation Step 3: Determine the Explanatory Power of the Model

The Adjusted R^2

When analyzing multiple regression models, the adjusted coefficient of determination (adj-R^2) is used rather than the unadjusted coefficient of determination (R^2) that is used in simple regression.[2] The reason for the

---

[2] The relationship between R^2 and adj-R^2 is $\text{adj-R}_2 = \dfrac{\left\{1-(1-R^2)\Big/_{n-1}\right\}}{\left\{^{n-1}\Big/_{n-(k+1)}\right\}}$

where n represents the number of observations and k represents the number of independent variables. If n is large relative to k there will be little difference between R^2 and adj-R^2.

adjustment is due to the fact that the unadjusted R^2 will always increase as *any* new independent variable is added to the model, whether the variable is relevant or not. On the other hand, the adj-R^2 may or may not increase when a new independent variable is added to the model. Thus, in interpreting multiple linear regression results one should always look at the adjusted coefficient of determination (adj-R^2) in order to evaluate the explanatory power of the model. The adj-R^2 still *gives the percentage of the variation in the dependent variable (Y) that is explained by the regression model.*

For the Stoke's Lodge hotel occupancy model, the adjusted coefficient of determination is 0.201 (see Table 6.2).[3] This means that 20.1% of the variation in monthly room occupancy (the dependent variable) is explained by the model (variation in the independent variables). In the bivariate (simple) regression in Chapter 4 for Stoke's Lodge you saw that the explanatory power was only 14.8%. Now you see that by adding an additional independent variable the explanatory power has increased to 20.1%. In an appendix to Chapter 8 you will see that this can be improved to about 83%.

Overall Test of Significance for Multiple Regression

A test of the overall significance of a regression equation can be performed for multiple regression and is related to the coefficient of determination. It is sometimes referred to as the F-test. The null hypothesis is that there is no relationship between the dependent variable and the set of all independent variables. That is, $H_0 : \beta_1 = \beta_2 = \ldots = \beta_k = 0$ (i.e., all slope terms are simultaneously equal to zero).[4] The alternative hypothesis is that all slope terms are not simultaneously equal to zero and denoted by H_1: At least one $\beta_i \neq 0$.[5]

---

[3] Again, one would rarely calculate the adjusted coefficient of determination manually. It will generally be given in the computer printout and is most often identified as "Adjusted R Squared" or "adj-R^2."

[4] This is equivalent to the null hypothesis that R^2 (or adj-R^2) is equal to 0.

[5] This is equivalent to the alternative hypothesis that R^2 (or adj-R^2) is not equal to 0.

The computed test statistic for the test of overall significance is the F-statistic, Fc, and can be computed as follows:

$$F_c = \frac{\left\{\dfrac{SSR}{k}\right\}}{\left[\dfrac{SSE}{n-(k+1)}\right]}$$

where SSR is the sum of squared regression (explained variation) and measures the amount of the variation in the dependent variable (Y) that is explained by the set of independent variables; SSE is the sum of squared residuals, or errors (unexplained variation), and measures the amount of the variation in the dependent variable (Y) that is explained by one or more variables not considered in our regression model; k is the number of independent variables in the model; and n is the total number of observations in the sample. The computed F-statistic, F_c, can be found as a standard part of most computer regression outputs. Table 6.2 shows that F_c is equal to 13.567 for the Stoke's Lodge multiple regression example. You see, in Table 6.2, that this statistic is part of an "ANOVA" table. ANOVA refers to analysis of variance, which is another statistical tool.

The critical value for the F-test can be found using the F-distribution table (F-table for a 5% level of significance is shown in Appendix 6A). The appropriate degrees of freedom (df) for the F-test are equal to k for the numerator and $n - (k + 1)$ for the denominator. The critical value is then found at the intersection of the column and row corresponding to these values. In the Stoke's Lodge multiple regression example, the df for the numerator is equal to $k = 2$ and the df for the denominator is equal to $n - (k + 1) = 101 - (2 + 1) = 98$. So, the critical F-table value is 3.07.[6]

If the computed F-statistic, F_c, is greater than or equal to the critical value from the F-table (this is always a right-tailed test), the null hypothesis is rejected. Also, note that a p-value is given in the Excel computer output next to the computed F-statistic. If the p-value is less than or equal to the desired level of significance, α, this also tells you that the null hypothesis

---

[6] The denominator df of 98 is not given on the F-table in Appendix 6A. Therefore, you can approximate it using the closest value for the denominator df, which in this case is 120.

can be rejected. If the null hypothesis is rejected, you can conclude that overall the regression function does show a statistically significant relationship between the dependent variable and the set of independent variables. In the case of Stoke's Lodge, the computed F_c (13.567) is greater than the critical F-table value (3.07) and/or the p-value (0.000) is less than the desired level of significance (0.05). Therefore, the null hypothesis is rejected and you conclude that overall the regression model is significant at a 95 percent confidence level.

Evaluation Step 4: Check for Serial Correlation

The procedure used to check for serial correlation in multiple regression analysis is exactly the same as described in Chapter 4 for simple regression analysis. There is no difference! Recall, since MRO is time-series data, a check for serial correlation is necessary for the Stoke's Lodge multiple regression example. The DW statistic is calculated to be 0.7303.

To formally evaluate the DW statistic for the MRO regression you know that $n = 101$ (number of observations) and $k = 2$ (number of independent variables). From the DW table (Appendix 4C), you find the lower bound of DW = 1.391 and the upper bound of DW = 1.600.[7] Test 6 in Table 4.2 is satisfied, since the calculated DW statistic of 0.7303 is less than the lower bound (1.391) from the DW table. Therefore, positive serial correlation still exists in the multiple regression model for MRO.[8] Remember that serial correlation does not affect the regression coefficients but can inflate the computed t-ratios (t_c).

Evaluation Step 5: Check for Multicollinearity

Multicollinearity occurs when two or more of the independent variables in multiple regression are highly correlated with one another. When multicollinearity exists, the regression results may not be reliable in that

---

[7] The DW table in Appendix 4C only goes up to 40 observations. So, you can approximate with that value.

[8] In the Appendix to Chapter 8, you will see that in a more complete model for Stoke's Lodge the DW statistic can be increased to 1.883.

the values of the slope terms may be incorrectly estimated. The existence of multicollinearity may be a reason why the signs of the slope terms in a model fail to make logical sense. This would be an example of *overspecification* of a regression model.

When multicollinearity exists, it does not necessarily mean that the regression function cannot be useful. The individual coefficients may not be reliable, but as a group they are likely to contain compensating errors. One may be too high, but another is likely to be too low (even to the extreme of having signs that are the opposite of your expectations). As a result, if your *only* interest is in using the regression for prediction, the entire function may perform satisfactorily. However, you could not use the model to evaluate the influence of individual independent variables on the dependent variable. Thus, one would rarely, if ever, use a model for which multicollinearity was a problem.

Two readily observable factors might indicate the existence of a multicollinearity problem. One indicator is that the standard errors of the slope terms are large (inflated) relative to the estimated slope terms. This results in an unacceptably low computed t-statistics, t_c, for variables that you expect to be statistically significant. A second indication of a multicollinearity problem occurs when pairs of independent variables have high correlation coefficients. It is therefore important to examine the correlation coefficients for all pairs of independent variables included in the regression. Generally, you should avoid using pairs of independent variables that have simple correlation coefficients (in absolute value) above 0.7. However, in practice, using data for economic and business analyses, this is sometimes a high standard to achieve. As a result, you might end up using pairs of variables that have a slightly higher correlation coefficient than 0.7 if everything else in the model is acceptable.

Some things can be done to reduce multicollinearity problems. One is to use constant dollar terms when using money values. This removes the simultaneous effect of inflation from money-measured variables. You might also remove all but one of the highly correlated variables from the regression to reduce multicollinearity.

The simple correlation coefficient between monthly gas price (GP) and monthly casino employees (CE), the two independent variables in the MRO regression model, is found to be –0.023.[9] This value is well below 0.7 in absolute value so multicollinearity does not seem to be an issue in the Stoke's Lodge multiple regression model.

Point and Interval Estimates for Multiple Regression

The procedure for finding point and interval estimates of the value of the dependent variable in a multiple regression model is almost identical to simple regression. The only exception is that in multiple regression analysis the point estimate of the dependent variable is based on the values of multiple independent variables. To illustrate, consider the multiple regression model for Stoke's Lodge where monthly room occupancy (MRO) was a function of monthly gas price (GP) and monthly casino employees (CE). Suppose that you wanted to estimate MRO for next month when you think the GP will be $3.65 per gallon and expect 6,800 employees working in casinos (remember CEs are in thousands).

You can make this point estimate by substituting these values of the independent variables (GP and CE) into the regression model as follows:

$$MRO = 15{,}484.483 - 1{,}097.686(GP) - 1{,}013.646(CE)$$
$$MRO = 15{,}484.483 - 1{,}097.686(3.65) - 1{,}013.646(6.8) = 4{,}585.136$$

Thus, when average monthly gas price is $3.65 per gallon and there are 6,800 employees working in casinos in the state, the estimated monthly room occupancy at Stoke's Lodge would be 4,585.

You can also calculate the approximate 95 percent confidence interval for the previous point estimate. The point estimate is 4,585.136 and the SEE is 1,611.772. The approximate 95 percent confidence interval is:

$$Point\ Estimate \pm 2(SEE)$$
$$4{,}585.136 \pm 2(1{,}611.772) =$$
$$4{,}585.136 \pm 3{,}223.544 =$$
$$1{,}361.592\ to\ 7{,}808.680$$

---

[9] Correlation coefficients can be easily calculated in Excel (see Chapter 3).

Therefore, you are 95 percent confident that monthly room occupancy at Stoke's Lodge will be between 1,362 and 7,809 if the average monthly gas price is $3.65 per gallon and there are 6,800 employees working in casinos.

One Last Look at the Stoke's Lodge Multiple Regression Model

The graph in Figure 6.2 shows one final look at the Stoke's Lodge multiple regression model evaluated in this chapter. The predicted line captures the downward trend in the model. However, it does not capture the seasonality that is present in the actual data. In Chapter 8, you will learn to capture seasonal variation with the use of qualitative dummy variables that will greatly improve this model.

Summary and Looking Ahead

In this chapter you have learned the difference between simple and multiple linear regression analysis. You have learned how to apply the five-step procedure used to evaluate a multiple regression model. First, it is necessary to determine whether the model makes logical sense. Second,

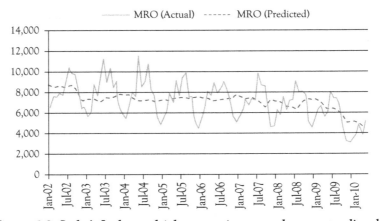

Figure 6.2 Stoke's Lodge multiple regression: actual versus predicted regression estimates. The line representing the predicted MRO for Stoke's Lodge is the dashed line derived from the following regression model: MRO = 15,484.483 − 1,097.686(GP) − 1,013.646(CE)

you should check for statistical significance of the slope terms for all independent variables. You now know a new "p-value" method that can be used to determine statistical significance. Third, you can determine the explanatory power of the model by evaluating the adjusted coefficient of determination or adj-R^2. You learned a new hypothesis test that is related to the coefficient of determination that tests the overall significance of the regression model. Next, if you have time-series data, you need to check for serial correlation. Finally, you need to check for multicollinearity between independent variables. As you read through the rest of the book you will use this procedure to evaluate multiple regression models. Specifically, in Chapter 7, you will apply this five-step procedure to a market share multiple regression example. Then, in Chapter 8, you will build upon your understanding of multiple regression analysis by including qualitative independent variables in the model. In Chapter 10, you will analyze the development and evaluation of two additional multiple regression models that include sales at Abercrombie & Fitch as well as U.S. retail jewelry sales.

What You Have Learned in Chapter 6

- To identify the five steps involved in evaluating a multiple regression model.
- To evaluate whether a multiple regression model makes logical sense.
- To check for statistical significance of all slope terms in a multiple regression model.
- To use the p-value method to evaluate statistical significance.
- To evaluate the explanatory power of a multiple regression model.
- To test the overall significance of a multiple regression model.
- To check for serial correlation in multiple regression models with time-series data.
- To check for multicollinearity in multiple regression models.
- To make a point and interval estimate based on a multiple regression model.

Appendix 6A: Critical Values of the
F-distribution at a 95 Percent Confidence Level

Degrees of Freedom for the Numerator $= k$

*	1	2	3	4	5	6	7	8	9
1	161.4	199.5	215.7	224.6	230.2	234.0	236.8	238.9	240.5
2	18.51	19.00	19.16	19.25	19.30	19.33	19.35	19.37	19.38
3	10.13	9.55	9.28	9.12	9.01	8.94	8.89	8.85	8.81
4	7.71	6.94	6.59	6.39	6.26	6.16	6.09	6.04	6.00
5	6.61	5.79	5.41	5.19	5.05	4.95	4.88	4.82	4.77
6	5.99	5.14	4.76	4.53	4.39	4.28	4.21	4.15	4.10
7	5.59	4.74	4.35	4.12	3.97	3.87	3.79	3.73	3.68
8	5.32	4.46	4.07	3.84	3.69	3.58	3.50	3.44	3.39
9	5.12	4.26	3.86	3.63	3.48	3.37	3.29	3.23	3.18
10	4.96	4.10	3.71	3.48	3.33	3.22	3.14	3.07	3.02
11	4.84	3.98	3.59	3.36	3.20	3.09	3.01	2.95	2.90
12	4.75	3.89	3.49	3.26	3.11	3.00	2.91	2.85	2.80
13	4.67	3.81	3.41	3.18	3.03	2.92	2.83	2.77	2.71
14	4.60	3.74	3.34	3.11	2.96	2.85	2.76	2.70	2.65
15	4.54	3.68	3.29	3.06	2.90	2.79	2.71	2.64	2.59
16	4.49	3.63	3.24	3.01	2.85	2.74	2.66	2.59	2.54
17	4.45	3.59	3.20	2.96	2.81	2.70	2.61	2.55	2.49
18	4.41	3.55	3.16	2.93	2.77	2.66	2.58	2.51	2.46
19	4.38	3.52	3.13	2.90	2.74	2.63	2.54	2.48	2.42
20	4.35	3.49	3.10	2.87	2.71	2.60	2.51	2.45	2.39
21	4.32	3.47	3.07	2.84	2.68	2.57	2.49	2.42	2.37
22	4.30	3.44	3.05	2.82	2.66	2.55	2.46	2.40	2.34
23	4.28	3.42	3.03	2.80	2.64	2.53	2.44	2.37	2.32
24	4.26	3.40	3.01	2.78	2.62	2.51	2.42	2.36	2.30
25	4.24	3.39	2.99	2.76	2.60	2.49	2.40	2.34	2.28
26	4.23	3.37	2.98	2.74	2.59	2.47	2.39	2.32	2.27
27	4.21	3.35	2.96	2.73	2.57	2.46	2.37	2.31	2.25
28	4.20	3.34	2.95	2.71	2.56	2.45	2.36	2.29	2.24
29	4.18	3.33	2.93	2.70	2.55	2.43	2.35	2.28	2.22
30	4.17	3.32	2.92	2.69	2.53	2.42	2.33	2.27	2.21
40	4.08	3.23	2.84	2.61	2.45	2.34	2.25	2.18	2.12
60	4.00	3.15	2.76	2.53	2.37	2.25	2.17	2.10	2.04
120	3.92	3.07	2.68	2.45	2.29	2.17	2.09	2.02	1.96
∞	3.84	3.00	2.60	2.37	2.21	2.10	2.01	1.94	1.88

* Degrees of freedom for the denominator (n) are shown in the far left column.

Critical Values of the F-Distribution at a 95 Percent Confidence Level (Continued)

Degrees of Freedom for the Numerator = k

10	12	15	20	24	30	40	60	120	∞
241.9	243.9	245.9	248.0	249.1	250.1	251.1	252.2	253.3	254.3
19.40	19.41	19.43	19.45	19.45	19.46	19.47	19.48	19.49	19.50
8.79	8.74	8.70	8.66	8.64	8.62	8.59	8.57	8.55	8.53
5.96	5.91	5.86	5.80	5.77	5.75	5.72	5.69	5.66	5.63
4.74	4.68	4.62	4.56	4.53	4.50	4.46	4.43	4.40	4.36
4.06	4.00	3.94	3.87	3.84	3.81	3.77	3.74	3.70	3.67
3.64	3.57	3.51	3.44	3.41	3.38	3.34	3.30	3.27	3.23
3.35	3.28	3.22	3.15	3.12	3.08	3.04	3.01	2.97	2.93
3.14	3.07	3.01	2.94	2.90	2.86	2.83	2.79	2.75	2.71
2.98	2.91	2.85	2.77	2.74	2.70	2.66	2.62	2.58	2.54
2.85	2.79	2.72	2.65	2.61	2.57	2.53	2.49	2.45	2.40
2.75	2.69	2.62	2.54	2.51	2.47	2.43	2.38	2.34	2.30
2.67	2.60	2.53	2.46	2.42	2.38	2.34	2.30	2.25	2.21
2.60	2.53	2.46	2.39	2.35	2.31	2.27	2.22	2.18	2.13
2.54	2.48	2.40	2.33	2.29	2.25	2.20	2.16	2.11	2.07
2.49	2.42	2.35	2.28	2.24	2.19	2.15	2.11	2.06	2.01
2.45	2.38	2.31	2.23	2.19	2.15	2.10	2.06	2.01	1.96
2.41	2.34	2.27	2.19	2.15	2.11	2.06	2.02	1.97	1.92
2.38	2.31	2.23	2.16	2.11	2.07	2.03	1.98	1.93	1.88
2.35	2.28	2.20	2.12	2.08	2.04	1.99	1.95	1.90	1.84
2.32	2.25	2.18	2.10	2.05	2.01	1.96	1.92	1.87	1.81
2.30	2.23	2.15	2.07	2.03	1.98	1.94	1.89	1.84	1.78
2.27	2.20	2.13	2.05	2.01	1.96	1.91	1.86	1.81	1.76
2.25	2.18	2.11	2.03	1.98	1.94	1.89	1.84	1.79	1.73
2.24	2.16	2.09	2.01	1.96	1.92	1.87	1.82	1.77	1.71
2.22	2.15	2.07	1.99	1.95	1.90	1.85	1.80	1.75	1.69
2.20	2.13	2.06	1.97	1.93	1.88	1.84	1.79	1.73	1.67
2.19	2.12	2.04	1.96	1.91	1.87	1.82	1.77	1.71	1.65
2.18	2.10	2.03	1.94	1.90	1.85	1.81	1.75	1.70	1.64
2.16	2.09	2.01	1.93	1.89	1.84	1.79	1.74	1.68	1.62
2.08	2.00	1.92	1.84	1.79	1.74	1.69	1.64	1.58	1.51
1.99	1.92	1.84	1.75	1.70	1.65	1.59	1.53	1.47	1.39
1.91	1.83	1.75	1.66	1.61	1.55	1.50	1.43	1.35	1.25
1.83	1.75	1.67	1.57	1.52	1.46	1.39	1.32	1.22	1.00

Source: Modified from, NIST/SEMATECH e-Handbook of Statistical Methods, http://www.itl.nist.gov/div898/handbook/, February 6, 2012.

CHAPTER 7

A Market Share Multiple Regression Model

Chapter 7 Preview

When you have completed reading this chapter you will be able to:

- Identify what constitutes a market share multiple regression model.
- Arrange your data for use in a market share multiple regression model.
- Determine whether a particular variable ought to be in the model.
- Evaluate the market share model.
- Make a point estimate from the model.
- Calculate a confidence interval for your estimate.

In the previous chapters, you have seen examples of simple linear regressions (those with a single independent variable) and multiple linear regressions (those with more than one independent variable). Now, you will apply these concepts of regression analysis to estimate a model for the market share of a company. Table 7.1 contains the data used in this example: three years of quarterly data related to the market share for Miller's Foods. The objective is to develop a regression model that explains how Miller's Foods' price (P) and advertising (AD), as well as an index of competitors' advertising (CAD), have influenced the firm's market share (MS).

Table 7.1 Three years of Miller's Foods' market share multiple regression data

Period (quarter)	Market share in M$ (MS)	Price in $ (P)	Advertising in $ (AD)	Competitors' advertising index (CAD)
1	19	5.20	500	11
2	17	5.32	550	11
3	14	5.48	550	12
4	15	5.60	550	12
5	18	5.80	550	9
6	16	6.03	660	10
7	16	6.01	615	10
8	19	5.92	650	10
9	23	5.90	745	9
10	27	5.85	920	10
11	23	5.80	1,053	11
12	21	5.85	950	11

Source: Proprietary data.

Estimating a Simple Linear Regression Market Share Model

It would be reasonable to assume that the market share for MF would be related to their price variable. If you estimate a simple linear regression to represent this assumption, using only price as an independent variable, you receive the following result (MS as a function of P):

$$MS = -2.047 + 3.673(P)$$

This is a rather disappointing result in at least two dimensions. First, this estimated coefficient for price (+3.673) has a positive sign! How would you interpret this? The positive sign and the value of 3.673 infer that if price were to increase by one, market share would increase by 3.673 (measured in percentage terms, thus 3.673%). That is a very unusual result to say the least. If this is correct, you could increase the market share (a good thing) by simply raising prices. But is this logical? No! This clearly violates the economic Law of Demand which states that "if you change nothing else other than raising price, sales, or quantity demanded, will decrease." Secondly, the t-stat on the coefficient of the independent variable (price) is far below the "rule-of-thumb" value of 2; this would infer that the estimated coefficient (+3.673) is not significantly different from zero. In other words, the coefficient is not statistically significant; it is not a reliable coefficient and you should be suspect of using it in any manner even if it was logical. Note that if the coefficient is actually zero (and that could very well be the case with this computed test statistic) there is no demonstrated relationship between price and sales. The inference would be that raising price has no effect on sales! That also is a very unlikely occurrence.

So, this model should not be used. Is the regression result incorrect? No, the estimated regression result is accurate, but you may have made an incorrect assumption by constricting the regression model to relate market share to only a single independent variable. In statistical terms we might say that the "form" of the regression model is incorrect; it does not appear to mimic what is taking place in the real world. It appears that in the real world of MF, market share depends upon more than just price (the model is underspecified). That is the reason you use multiple linear regression; you recognize that not only price is important in determining market share, but also their advertising effort, and some measure of their competitors' advertising effort. Leaving out important explanatory variables will affect the coefficients of the remaining variables and "cloud" the picture you receive of the way each affects the dependent variable. There are many variables that affect the sales at Miller's Foods and we know we will not be able to include every one of them, but we do need to include those that have the most effect on sales.

Estimating a Multiple Linear Regression Market Share Model

Putting this disappointing simple linear regression result away, you can estimate a multiple linear regression using three independent variables: price (P), advertising (AD), and an index of their competitors' advertising (CAD). This is based on the assumption that these are the three most important variables affecting Miller's Food sales.

Table 7.2 Excel regression results for Miller's Foods' market share model

Regression Statistics					
Multiple R	0.929		DW = 2.17		
R-square	0.863				
Adjusted R-square	0.812				
Standard error	1.676				
Observations	12				
ANOVA					
	df	*SS*	*MS*	*F*	*Sig F*
Regression	3	141.537	47.179	16.802	0.001
Residual	8	22.463	2.808		
Total	11	164			
	Coefficients	*Std error*	*t Stat*	*p-Value*	*P/2*
Intercept	80.011	19.479	4.107	0.003	0.002
P	−8.458	2.705	−3.127	0.014	0.007
AD	0.020	0.003	6.404	0.000	0.000
CAD	−2.541	0.647	−3.924	0.004	0.002

The Excel regression results for this example are summarized in Table 7.2. From the results given in Table 7.2, you could write the estimated regression equation as:

$$MS = 80.011 - 8.458(P) + 0.020(AD) - 2.541(CAD)$$

Evaluating the Estimated Market Share Model

In order to complete the examination of this model, you should use the five-step process described previously (see Chapter 6) to evaluate multiple regression models.

Evaluation Step 1: Evaluate Whether the Model Makes Sense

Does the model make sense? The signs on the coefficients for all three independent variables do make economic sense as described next.

The interpretation of the slope terms for price, advertising, and the competitors' advertising index are as follows:

1. Price. The coefficient −8.458 has a negative sign, which indicates that as price goes up, market share goes down. Note that this is different from the sign you received in the simple linear regression. The negative sign makes economic sense; it implies that for every $1 increase in price, market share is expected to fall by 8.458 market share percentage points; or for every 10 cent increase in price, market share would be expected to fall by .8458 market share percentage points. The relationship is symmetric. Price cuts would be expected to increase market share by like amounts.

2. Advertising. The coefficient 0.02 has a positive sign, which indicates that increasing advertising is expected to increase market share. This result also follows economic reasoning. With everything else held constant we should expect that expenditures on advertising would have a positive effect on sales. Each $100 increase in advertising is expected to increase market share by 2.0 market share percentage points. Again, the result is assumed to be symmetric. Decreases in advertising would lower market share in a like manner.

3. Index of Competitors' Advertising. The negative sign for the index indicates that this firm's market share would fall when competitors advertise more. This is also what we would expect from economic theory; with everything else held constant, if our competitor ramps us advertising, we should expect to see a dip in our sales. Every 1 unit rise in the index is expected to lower market share by 2.541 market share percentage points. Decreases in the index would be expected to increase market share in a like manner.

Therefore, this model passes our test for sound business/economic logic.

Evaluation Step 2: Check for Statistical Significance

Are the slope terms significantly different from zero? That is, does each of the independent variables have a statistically significant influence on the dependent variable? The hypotheses you would want to evaluate for each of the slope terms are as follows:

For price (Case 2)	$H_0 : \beta_1 \geq 0,$	$H_1 : \beta_1 < 0$
For advertising (Case 3)	$H_0 : \beta_2 \leq 0,$	$H_1 : \beta_2 > 0$
For Comp. Ad (Case 2)	$H_0 : \beta_3 \leq 0,$	$H_1 : \beta_3 < 0$

These all imply a one-tailed test. From the t-table presented earlier (Appendix 4B), you find that the critical value of t at 8 degrees of freedom (df $= 12 - (3 + 1) = 8$) and a 95 percent confidence level (5 percent confidence level) for a one-tailed test is 1.860. Thus,

1. For price, you reject H_0, since the absolute value of $t_c(|-3.13|)$ is greater than the critical t-table value (1.860). This implies that the coefficient for price is statistically less than zero.
2. For advertising, you reject H_0, since the absolute value of $t_c(|6.40|)$ is greater than the critical t-table value (1.860). This implies that the coefficient for advertising is statistically greater than zero.
3. For competitors' advertising, the absolute value of $t_c(|-3.92|)$ is greater than the critical t-table value (1.860). This implies that the coefficient for competitors' advertising is statistically less than zero.

Two of the computed test statistics are negative (the one on price and the one on competitors' advertising). This is not abnormal; a t-stat will always be negative when the coefficient is negative. We always evaluate the absolute value of the t-statistic as we have done above. Also, note that, in Table 7.2, all the p-values divided by 2 (relevant for one tailed tests) are far below the desired level of significance (0.05) also implying statistical significance.

Based on rejecting all three of these null hypotheses you conclude, at a 95 percent confidence level, that all three independent variables have a significant effect on the market share of Miller's Foods. In other words, you can rely on the three coefficients and use them in describing how Miller's market share is affected by each of the variables. We are confident that the real values of the coefficients are not equal to zero and that the best estimate of the actual value is the one given by the regression equation. Note that when you ran the simple linear regression with only price as an independent variable, you were not able to rely on the estimated slope of the price variable. That is, it was somewhat likely that that the true value of the price coefficient was zero. What has changed? The market share and price variables are identical in the simple regression and the multiple regression. But, what has changed is the addition of the two independent variables in the multiple regression; the multiple linear regression recognizes that market share is not only dependent upon price, but it is also dependent upon advertising and competitors' advertising at the same time. It is the "form" of the equation that has changed; we now believe this is a more accurate representation of what takes place in the real world and that the estimated coefficients tell us how each variable independently affects Miller's sales.

Evaluation Step 3: Determine Explanatory Power of Model

How much of the variation (i.e., "up and down movement") in Miller's Foods' market share does this regression model explain? In other words, how much of the variation in sales is due to the variation in price, the variation in advertising, and the variation in Miller's competitors' advertising? Because this is a multiple linear regression model you want to use the adjusted R^2 to answer this question. Recall that it is adjusted for the degrees of freedom lost when we added two additional explanatory variables. From Table 7.2, you see that the adjusted R^2 is 0.812. Thus, over 81 percent of the variation in Miller's Foods' market share (MS) is explained by this model. You can infer that most of the change you see in market share over the three years for which you have data is due to changes in price, advertising, and Miller's competitors' advertising. There are in fact other variables that effect Miller's sales but these three account for most (81 percent) of the variation.

You can also use the F-test to evaluate the overall statistical significance of this model. The calculated F-statistic from Table 7.2 is compared with the critical F-table value (Appendix 6A) at k degrees of freedom for the numerator and $n - (k + 1)$ degrees of freedom for the denominator. In this example for the numerator df = 3 and the denominator df = 8. From the F-table (Appendix 6A) you see that the critical F-table value is 4.07.

Since the computed F-statistic from Table 7.2 (16.8) is greater than the critical F-table value (4.07) you would reject the null hypothesis that all of the slope terms are simultaneously equal to zero (or alternatively that the adjusted R^2 equals zero). Thus, this full regression test infers that the estimated relationships are reasonably accurate.

Evaluation Step 4: Check for Serial Correlation

You need to check for serial correlation because the Miller's Foods' Market Share regression uses time-series data. To do this, you need to evaluate the Durbin–Watson statistic explained previously. Your calculated value is DW = 2.17 (refer to Appendix 4D on how to calculate the DW statistic). Recall that the DW values may range from 0 to 4. If the DW is exactly 2, there is little chance of serial correlation. However, if the calculated DW is close to 0, or close to 4, the chance of serial correlation is high. A short-cut (or an approximation) often used by practitioners is to examine whether the DW statistic is between 1.5 and 2.5. If the calculated value is between these limits, you might assume that serial correlation is not a serious problem. In this case, the calculated value for DW of 2.17 is between dl (0.368) and du (2.287) of the DW table (Appendix 4C). This satisfies Test 5 of Table 4.2, so the result is actually indeterminate.

Evaluation Step 5: Check for Multicollinearity

You should evaluate the model for possible multicollinearity since you have multiple independent variables in the regression. This step is necessary if you are using more than one independent variable (as we are in this case). The signs for the coefficients all make sense and the t-ratios are all high so there is no suggestion on these grounds to suspect multicollinearity (the model does not appear to be overspecified). It is still, however, prudent to test for multicollinearity using the correlation coefficients. The correlation coefficients for all pairs of independent variables can be found in the correlation matrix in Table 7.3.

Obviously, each variable is perfectly correlated with itself (i.e., correlations of 1). Since none of the other correlation coefficients is particularly large (all below 0.7 in absolute value), it is unlikely that there is a significant multicollinearity problem in this regression.

Table 7.3 Correlation matrix for independent variables in Miller's Foods' market share regression

	P	AD	CAD
P	1		
AD	0.468	1	
CAD	−0.590	−0.092	1

Making an Estimate from the Market Share Model

Suppose you want to know what market share would be expected if MF set their price at $5.70 and spent $700 on advertising, and if the competitors' advertising index was expected to be 10 percent. You could make this point estimate by substituting these values into the regression model as follows:

$$MS = 80.011 - 8.458(P) + 0.020(AD) - 2.541(CAD)$$
$$MS = 80.011 - (8.458 \times 5.70) + (0.02 \times 700) - (2.541 \times 10)$$
$$MS = 20.39$$

The correctly calculated point estimate is a market share of 20.39, but how would you estimate an approximate 95 percent confidence interval for market share? From the Excel regression results in Table 7.2, you see that the standard error of the estimate (SEE) is 1.676. Thus, the approximate 95 percent confidence interval is

$$MS = 20.39 \pm (2 \times 1.676)$$
$$MS = 17.038 \text{ to } 23.742$$

This means that you would be 95 percent confident that the market share of Miller's Foods would fall in the interval from 17.038 percent through 23.742 percent if the firm set a $5.70 price and spent $700 on advertising, and if the competitors' advertising index was expected to be 10 percent.

The graph in Figure 7.1 further illustrates how well this regression model explains variations in MF's market share. You see that the estimated market share follows the actual market share quite well, except during the second quarter of the final year. You will learn more about this quarter in the next chapter.

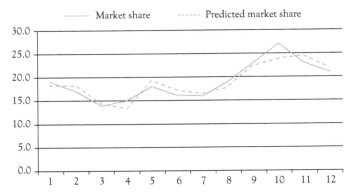

Figure 7.1 Miller's Foods' market share: actual and regression estimates. The dotted line representing the estimated market share for Miller's Foods' is derived from the following regression model:
MS = 80.011 − 8.458(P) + 0.020(AD) − 2.541(CAD)

A Three-Dimensional Visual Representation

To help you get a visual feel for what a multiple regression data set might look like, see the three-dimensional plot of market share, price, and advertising in Figure 7.2. You could not include the third independent variable in such a plot since the human mind cannot visualize beyond three dimensions. The regression plane for market share (MS) as a function of price (P) and advertising (AD) is shown in Figure 7.2. The equation for that plane is:

$$MS = 17.790 - 1.866(P) + 0.017(AD)$$

The actual data points in Figure 7.2 are shown by the dark circles and the regression plane is the shaded rectangle. Note that the estimated linear plane (this is the visual representation of the estimated regression equation) very closely approximates the placement of the data points on the scatterplot. The closer the data points in total to the regression plane, the better the regression R^2 or we could say, the better the fit of the regression. In this case the regression plane appears to be a very close fit to the data points.

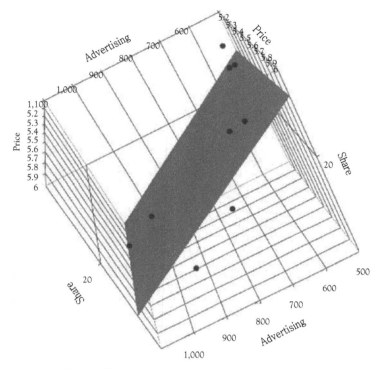

Figure 7.2 The market share multiple regression data 3D scatterplot. This figure shows the three-dimensional relationship between market share, price, and advertising

What You Have Learned in Chapter 7

- You know what constitutes a market share multiple regression model.
- You know how to arrange your data for use in a market share multiple regression model.
- You know how to determine whether a particular variable ought to be in the model.
- You know how to evaluate the market share model.
- You know how to make a point estimate from the model.
- You know how to estimate a confidence interval for your estimate.

CHAPTER 8

Qualitative Events and Seasonality in Multiple Regression Models

Chapter 8 Preview

When you have completed reading this chapter you will be able to:

- Understand the meaning of "seasonality" in business data.
- Take seasonality into account as a pattern in your models.
- Account for seasonality by using dummy variables.
- Understand the use of dummy variables to represent a wide range of events.
- Modify the Market Share model from Chapter 7 for a nonrecurring event.
- Use dummy variables to account for seasonality in women's clothing sales.

Introduction

Most of the variables you may want to use in developing a regression model are readily measurable with values that extend over a wide range and are interval or ratio data. All of the examples you have examined so far have involved variables of this type.

However, on occasion you may want to account for the effect of some event or attribute that has only two (or a few) possible cases. It either "is" or "is not" something. It either "has" or "does not have" some attribute. Some examples include the following: a month either is or is not June; a person either is or is not a woman; in a particular time period, there either was or was not a labor disturbance; a given quarter of the year either is or is not a second quarter; a teacher either has a doctorate or does not have one; a university either does or does not offer an MBA; and so forth.

The manner in which you can account for these noninterval and non-ratio data is by using dummy variables. The term "dummy" variable refers to the fact that this class of variable "dummies," or takes the place of, something you wish to represent that is not easily described by a more common numerical variable. A dummy variable (or several dummy variables) can be used to measure the effects of what may be qualitative attributes. A dummy variable is assigned a value of 1 or 0, depending on whether or not the particular observation has a given attribute. To explain the use of dummy variables consider two examples.

Another Look at Miller's Foods' Market Share Regression Model

The first example is an extension of the multiple linear regression discussed in Chapter 7 dealing with a model of Miller's Foods' market share (MS). In that situation, you saw a regression model in which the dependent variable MS was a function of three independent variables: price (P), advertising (AD), and an index of competitors' advertising (CAD). You saw the results of that regression in Table 7.2 and in Figure 7.1.

However, it so happens that in the second quarter of the third year (quarter 10), another major firm had a fire that significantly reduced its production and sales. As an analyst, you might suspect that this event could have influenced the MS of all firms for that period (including Miller's Foods). At the very least, it probably introduced some noise (error) into the data used for the regression and may have reduced the explanatory ability of the regression model.

You can use a dummy variable to account for the influence of the fire at the competitor's facility on Miller's Foods' MS and to measure its effect. To do so, you simply create a new variable—call it D—that has a value of 0 for every observation except the tenth quarter and a value of 1 for the tenth quarter. The data from Table 7.1 are reproduced in Table 8.1, but now include the addition of this dummy variable in the last column.

Table 8.1 *Twelve quarters (three years) of Miller's Foods' MS multiple regression data with the dummy variable*

Period	MS	P	AD	CAD	D
1	19	5.2	500	11	0
2	17	5.32	550	11	0
3	14	5.48	550	12	0
4	15	5.6	550	12	0
5	18	5.8	550	9	0
6	16	6.03	660	10	0
7	16	6.01	615	10	0
8	19	5.92	650	10	0
9	23	5.9	745	9	0
10	27	5.85	920	10	1
11	23	5.8	1,053	11	0
12	21	5.85	950	11	0

Using the data from Table 8.1 in a multiple regression analysis, you get the following equation for MS:

$$MS = 72.908 - 7.453(P) + .017(AD) - 2.245(CAD) + 4.132(D)$$

The complete regression results are shown in Table 8.2. You see that the coefficient of the dummy variable representing the fire is 4.132. The fact that it is positive indicates that when there was a fire at a major competitor's facility, the market share (MS) of Miller's Foods increased. This certainly makes sense. In addition, you can say that this event accounted for 4.132 of the 27 percent MS obtained during that second quarter of Year 3.

You should compare these regression results with those from Table 7.2. Note particularly the following:

1. The adjusted R-squared increased from 0.812 to 0.906.
2. The standard error of the regression (SEE) fell from 1.676 to 1.183.

You see that the regression with the dummy variable is considerably better than the first model presented in Chapter 7. This is further

Table 8.2 Miller's Foods' MS regression results including a dummy variable

Regression Statistics					
Multiple R	0.970		DW = 1.83		
R-square	0.940				
Adjusted R-square	0.906				
Standard error	1.183				
Observations	12				
ANOVA					
	df	*SS*	*MS*	*F*	*Sig. F*
Regression	4	154.202	38.550	27.541	0.000
Residual	7	9.798	1.400		
Total	11	164			
	Coefficients	*Std. error*	*t Stat*	*p-Value*	*p/2*
Intercept	72.908	13.955	5.225	0.001	0.001
P	−7.453	1.939	−3.845	0.006	0.003
AD	0.017	0.002	7.045	0.000	0.000
CAD	−2.245	0.468	−4.802	0.002	0.001
D	4.132	1.374	3.008	0.020	0.010

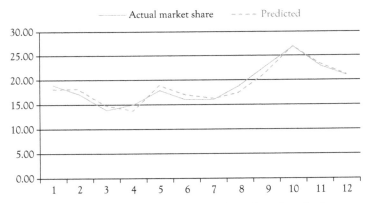

Figure 8.1 Miller's Foods' MS: actual and predicted with dummy variable. The line representing the estimated MS for Miller's Foods' is derived from the following regression model: MS = 72.908 − 7.453(P) + .017(AD) − 2.245(CAD) + 4.132(D)

illustrated by the graph in Figure 8.1, which shows the actual MS and the MS as estimated with the multiple regression model above. Comparing

Figure 8.1 with Figure 7.1 provides a good visual representation of how much the model is improved by adding the dummy variable to account for the abnormal influence in the tenth quarter.

Modeling the Seasonality of Womens' Clothing Sales

As a second example of the use of dummy variables, let's look at how they can be used to account for seasonality. Table 8.3 contains data for womens' clothing sales (WCS) on a monthly basis from January 2000 to December 2011. The full series of sales, from January 2000 to March 2001, is also graphed in Figure 8.2. You see in the graph that December sales are always high due to the heavy holiday sales experienced by most retailers, while January tends to have relatively low sales (when holiday giving turns to bill paying).

Eleven dummy variables can be used to identify and measure the seasonality in the firm's sales. In Table 8.3, you see that for each February observation the dummy variable February has a value of 1, but March and April are 0 (as are the dummy variables representing all the remaining months). Note that for each January none of the 11 dummy variables has a value of 1. That is because the first month (i.e., January) is not February, March, or any other month. Having a dummy variable for every month other than January makes January the base month for the model.

The dummy variables for the other months will then determine how much, on average, those months vary from the first month base period. Any of the 12 months could be selected as the base. In this example, January is selected as the base month because it is the lowest month of the year on average, after taking the upward trend in the data into account. Thus, you would expect the February, March, and April dummy variables to all have positive coefficients in the regression model.

First let's see what happens if you just estimate a simple regression using personal income (PI) as the only independent variable. The equation that results is:

$$WCS = 1,187.12 + 0.165(PI)$$

Table 8.3 Women's clothing sales (in M$) and 11 seasonal dummy variables. Only the first two years are shown so that you see how the dummy variables are set up

Date	WCS in M$	Feb	Mar	Apr	May	Jun	Jul	Aug	Sep	Oct	Nov	Dec
1/2000	1,683	0	0	0	0	0	0	0	0	0	0	0
2/2000	1,993	1	0	0	0	0	0	0	0	0	0	0
3/2000	2,673	0	1	0	0	0	0	0	0	0	0	0
4/2000	2,709	0	0	1	0	0	0	0	0	0	0	0
5/2000	2,812	0	0	0	1	0	0	0	0	0	0	0
6/2000	2,567	0	0	0	0	1	0	0	0	0	0	0
7/2000	2,385	0	0	0	0	0	1	0	0	0	0	0
8/2000	2,643	0	0	0	0	0	0	1	0	0	0	0
9/2000	2,660	0	0	0	0	0	0	0	1	0	0	0
10/2000	2,651	0	0	0	0	0	0	0	0	1	0	0
11/2000	2,826	0	0	0	0	0	0	0	0	0	1	0
12/2000	3,878	0	0	0	0	0	0	0	0	0	0	1
1/2001	1,948	0	0	0	0	0	0	0	0	0	0	0
2/2001	2,156	1	0	0	0	0	0	0	0	0	0	0
3/2001	2,673	0	1	0	0	0	0	0	0	0	0	0
4/2001	2,804	0	0	1	0	0	0	0	0	0	0	0
5/2001	2,750	0	0	0	1	0	0	0	0	0	0	0
6/2001	2,510	0	0	0	0	1	0	0	0	0	0	0
7/2001	2,313	0	0	0	0	0	1	0	0	0	0	0
8/2001	2,663	0	0	0	0	0	0	1	0	0	0	0
9/2001	2,397	0	0	0	0	0	0	0	1	0	0	0
10/2001	2,618	0	0	0	0	0	0	0	0	1	0	0
11/2001	2,790	0	0	0	0	0	0	0	0	0	1	0
12/2001	3,865	0	0	0	0	0	0	0	0	0	0	1

This function is plotted in the top graph of Figure 8.2 along with the raw sales data. As you can see, the estimate goes roughly through the center of the data without coming very close to any month's actual sales on a consistent basis.

Now if you add the 11 dummy variables to the regression model, the multiple regression model that results is:

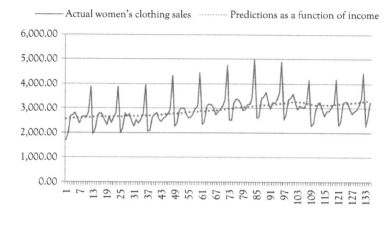

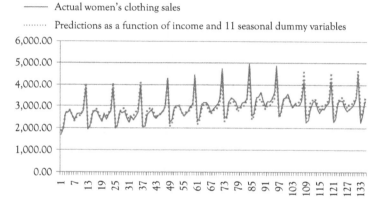

Figure 8.2 *Women's clothing sales data. Compare these two graphs to see how helpful the dummy variables for seasonality can be*

$$WCS = 572.16 + 0.16(PI) + 147.36(Feb) + 765.96(Mar)$$
$$+ 859.48(Apr) + 900.81(May) + 631.60(Jun) + 411.26(Jul)$$
$$+ 584.74(Aug) + 579.07(Sep) + 701.99(Oct) + 901.60(Nov)$$
$$+ 2,094.95(Dec)$$

Now look at the lower graph in Figure 8.2 which shows estimated sales based on a model that includes PI and the 11 monthly dummy variables superimposed on the actual sales pattern. In many months, the estimated series performs so well that the two cannot be distinguished from one another. The complete regression results for this model are found in Table 8.4.

Table 8.4 Regression results for WCS with seasonal dummy variables

Regression Statistics					
Multiple R	0.963		DW = 0.52		
R-square	0.927				
Adjusted R-square	0.919				
Standard error	163.410				
Observations	135				
ANOVA					
	df	SS	MS	F	Sig F
Regression	12	41,101,414	3,425,118	128.269	0.000
Residual	122	3,257,726.8	26,702.68		
Total	134	44,359,141			
	Coefficients	Std. error	t Stat	p-Value	p/2
Intercept	572.163	113.464	5.043	0.000	0.000
PI	0.157	0.010	16.061	0.000	0.000
Feb	147.356	66.712	2.209	0.029	0.015
Mar	765.957	66.715	11.481	0.000	0.000
Apr	859.476	68.218	12.599	0.000	0.000
May	900.811	68.212	13.206	0.000	0.000
Jun	631.599	68.211	9.259	0.000	0.000
Jul	411.262	68.211	6.029	0.000	0.000
Aug	584.738	68.212	8.572	0.000	0.000
Sep	579.067	68.213	8.489	0.000	0.000
Oct	701.994	68.216	10.291	0.000	0.000
Nov	901.599	68.219	13.216	0.000	0.000
Dec	2,094.946	68.232	30.703	0.000	0.000

The interpretation of the regression coefficients for the seasonal dummy variables is straightforward. Remember that as this model is constructed, the first month (January) is the base period. Thus, the coefficients for the dummy variables can be interpreted as follows:

- For the February dummy the regression coefficient 147.356 indicates that on average February sales are $147.356 million above January (base period) sales.

- For the March dummy the regression coefficient 765.957 indicates that on average March sales are $765.957 million above January (base period) sales.
- For the April dummy the regression coefficient 859.476 indicates that on average April sales are $859.476 million above January (base period) sales.

The remaining eight dummy variables would be interpreted in the same manner.

The regression coefficient for income (0.157) means that WCS are increasing at an average of $0.157 million for every billion dollar increase in PI. Note that WCS are denominated in millions of dollars while income is denominated in billions of dollars. Knowing the units of measurement for each variable is important.

Let's summarize some of the results of these two regression analyses of WCS:

	Without seasonal dummy variables	With seasonal dummy variables
R^2 and Adjusted R^2	0.167	0.919
F-Statistic	27.8	128.3
Standard error of regression (SEE)	525.16	163.41

The model that includes the dummy variables to account for seasonality is clearly the superior model based on these diagnostic measures. The better fit of the model can also be seen visually in Figure 8.2. However, the DW statistic (0.52) in the larger model does indicate the presence of positive serial correlation.

As you have seen, the development of a model such as this to account for seasonality is not difficult. Dummy variables are not only an easy way to account for seasonality; they can also be used effectively to account for many other effects that cannot be handled by ordinary continuous numeric variables.

The model for WCS can be further improved by adding two additional variables: (1) the University of Michigan Index of Consumer Sentiment (UMICS), which measures the attitude of consumers regarding the

Table 8.5 Regression results for WCS with the addition of the
UMICS and WUR and seasonal dummy variables

Regression Statistics					
Multiple R	0.985		DW = 1.29		
R-square	0.970				
Adjusted R-square	0.966				
Standard error	105.403				
Observations	135				
ANOVA					
	df	SS	MS	F	Sig F
Regression	14	43,025,964	3,073,283	276.628	0.000
Residual	120	1,333,176	11,110		
Total	134	44,359,141			
	Coefficients	Std. error	t Stat	P-value	p/2
Intercept	−493.609	208.160	−2.371	0.019	0.010
PI	0.240	0.010	24.092	0.000	0.000
WUR	−69.366	8.044	−8.624	0.000	0.000
UMICS	6.581	1.199	5.488	0.000	0.000
Feb	170.311	43.187	3.944	0.000	0.000
Mar	795.541	43.260	18.390	0.000	0.000
Apr	879.704	44.303	19.857	0.000	0.000
May	916.233	44.175	20.741	0.000	0.000
Jun	643.657	44.091	14.599	0.000	0.000
Jul	427.283	44.096	9.690	0.000	0.000
Aug	612.048	44.249	13.832	0.000	0.000
Sep	609.528	44.346	13.745	0.000	0.000
Oct	746.065	44.594	16.730	0.000	0.000
Nov	938.182	44.384	21.138	0.000	0.000
Dec	2,116.818	44.094	48.007	0.000	0.000

economy; and (2) the women's unemployment rate (WUR). Both the new variables are statistically significant and have the expected signs. It should be expected that as consumer confidence climbs, sales would also increase; the positive sign on the UMICS coefficient displays this characteristic. Likewise, as women's unemployment rises it could be expected that sales of women's clothing would decrease; the negative sign on the WUR is consistent with this belief. These results are reported in Table 8.5; note that the adjusted R-square has increased to 0.966. This model still has positive serial correlation so you would want to be cautious about the t-tests. However, since all the t-ratios are again quite large this may not be a problem. Also, because serial correlation does not bias the coefficients these can be correctly interpreted.

In the appendix to this chapter, you will see another complete example of how dummy variables can be used to account for seasonality in data. This example expands on the analysis of occupancy for the Stoke's Lodge model.

What You Have Learned in Chapter 8

- You understand the meaning of "seasonality" in business data.
- You can take seasonality into account as a pattern in your models.
- You know how to account for seasonality by using dummy variables.
- You understand the use of dummy variables to represent a wide range of events.
- You are able to modify the MS model from Chapter 7 for a nonrecurring event.
- You can use dummy variables to account for seasonality in WCS.

Appendix

Stoke's Lodge Final Regression Results

Introduction

Recall that the Stoke's Lodge Monthly Room Occupancy (MRO) series represents the number of rooms occupied per month in a large independent motel. As you can see in Figure 8A.1, there is a downward trend in occupancy and what appears to be seasonality. The owners wanted to evaluate the causes for the decline. During the time period being considered there was a considerable expansion in the number of casinos in the State, most of which had integrated lodging facilities. Also, gas prices (GP) were increasing. You have seen that multiple regression can be used to evaluate the degree and significance of these factors.

The Data

The dependent variable for this multiple regression analysis is MRO. These values are shown in Figure 8A.1 for the period from January 2002 to May 2010. You see sharp peaks that probably represent seasonality in occupancy. For a hotel in this location, December would be expected to be a slow month.

Management had concerns about the effect of rising gas prices (GP) on the willingness of people to drive to this location (there is no good public, train, or air transportation available). They also had concerns

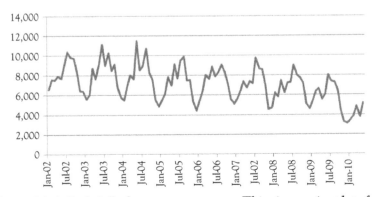

Figure 8A.1 Stoke's Lodge room occupancy. This time-series plot of occupancy for Stoke's Lodge appears to show considerable seasonality and a downward trend

about the influence that an increasing number of full service casino operations might have on their business because many of the casinos had integrated lodging facilities. Rather than use the actual number of casinos, the number of casino employees (CEs) is used to measure this influence because the casinos vary a great deal in size.

In Chapter 4, you saw the following model of monthly room occupancy (MRO) as a function of gas price (GP):

$$MRO = 9322.976 - 1080.448(GP)$$

You evaluated this model based on a four-step process and found it to be a pretty good model. The model was logical and statistically significant at a 95 percent confidence level. However, the coefficient of determination was only 14.8 percent ($R^2 = 0.148$) and the model had positive serial correlation (DW = 0.691).

In Chapter 6, you saw that the original model could be improved by adding the number of casino employees (CE) in the state. This yielded the following model:

$$MRO = 15,484.483 - 1,097.686(GP) - 1,013.646(CE)$$

This time you evaluated the model based on a five-step process because you had two independent variables rather than one, so needed to consider multicollinearity. Again the model seemed pretty good. The model was logical and statistically significant at a 95% confidence level. The coefficient of determination increased to 20.1% (Adjusted $R^2 = 0.201$). This model also had positive serial correlation (DW = 0.730). You will see that these results can be improved by using seasonal dummy variables.

A graph of the results from the model with just two independent variables is shown in Figure 8A.2. The dotted line representing the predictions follows the general downward movement of the actual occupancy. But what do you think is missing? Why are the residuals (errors) so large for most months? Do you think it could be because the model does not address the issue of seasonality in the data? If your answer is "yes" you are right. And, as with WCS, dummy variables can be used to deal with the seasonality issue.

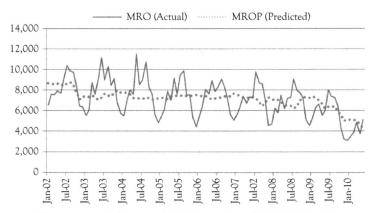

Figure 8A.2 Actual MRO and MRO predicted (MROP). The predicted values are shown by the dotted line, based on MRO as a function of GP and CE. The coefficient of determination for this model is 20.1 percent

The Hypotheses

When you estimate a regression you know that you have certain hypotheses in mind. In this case you know from Chapters 4 and 6 that you have the following hypotheses related to GP and CE.

$$H_0 : \beta \geq 0$$
$$H_1 : \beta < 0$$

That is, you have a research hypothesis that for both GP and CE the relationship with MRO is inverse. When either GP or CE increase you would expect MRO to decrease, so the alternative (research) hypothesis is that those slopes would be negative.

Based on conversations with Stoke's Lodge management, you can expect that December is their slowest month of the year on average. You can set up dummy variables for all months except December to test to see if this is true. Thus, for the dummy variables representing January–November the hypotheses would be:

$$H_0 : \beta \leq 0$$
$$H_1 : \beta > 0$$

This is due to the fact that you expect all dummy variables to be positive (by construction).

The first 15 months of data for this situation are shown in Table 8A.1. The regression results are shown in Table 8A.2.

The Results

From the regression output in Table 8A.2 you see some interesting results. First, the model follows the logic you would expect with negative coefficients for CP and CE, as well as positive coefficients for all 11 seasonal dummy variables. You also see from the F-test the as a whole the regression is very significant because the significance level (p-value) for F is 0.000. This means that you can be well over 95 percent confident that there is a significant relationship between MRO and the 13 independent variables in the model.

The t-ratios are all large enough that $p/2$ is less than the desired level of significance of 0.05 except for January and November. Recall that sometimes it is reasonable for you to drop your confidence level to 90 percent (a significance level of 10 percent, or 0.10). The coefficients for January and November satisfy this less stringent requirement. Look at the "Adjusted R-square" in Table 8A.2. It is 0.830, which tells you that this model explains about 83 percent of the variation in MRO for Stoke's Lodge. This is much better than the 20.1 percent you saw when seasonality was not considered.

In Table 8A.2, you also see that the DW statistic of 1.883 is now much closer to 2.0, the ideal value. Based on the abbreviated DW table in an appendix to Chapter 4, you would be restricted to using the row for 40 observations and the column for 10 independent variables. Doing so, you would conclude that the test is indeterminate. If you look online you can find more extensive DW tables.[1] For $n = 100$ and $k = 13$ you would find $d_l = 1.393$ and $d_u = 1.974$ in which case the result is still indeterminate.

To evaluate the possibility of multicollinearity, you need to look at the correlation matrix shown in Table 8A.3. There you see that all of the correlations are quite small so there is no multicollinearity problem with

---

[1] See: www.nd.edu/~wevans1/econ30331/Durbin_Watson_tables.pdf

Table 8A.1 The first 15 months of data. Notice the pattern of the values for the seasonal dummy variables. For each month in the "Date" column there is a one in the corresponding column representing that month

Date	MRO	GP	CE	Jan	Feb	Mar	Apr	May	June	July	Aug	Sept	Oct	Nov
Jan-02	6,575	1.35	5.3	1	0	0	0	0	0	0	0	0	0	0
Feb-02	7,614	1.46	5.2	0	1	0	0	0	0	0	0	0	0	0
Mar-02	7,565	1.55	5.2	0	0	1	0	0	0	0	0	0	0	0
Apr-02	7,940	1.45	5.2	0	0	0	1	0	0	0	0	0	0	0
May-02	7,713	1.52	5.1	0	0	0	0	1	0	0	0	0	0	0
Jun-02	9,110	1.81	5.0	0	0	0	0	0	1	0	0	0	0	0
Jul-02	10,408	1.57	5.0	0	0	0	0	0	0	1	0	0	0	0
Aug-02	9,862	1.45	5.0	0	0	0	0	0	0	0	1	0	0	0
Sep-02	9,718	1.60	5.1	0	0	0	0	0	0	0	0	1	0	0
Oct-02	8,354	1.57	5.8	0	0	0	0	0	0	0	0	0	1	0
Nov-02	6,442	1.56	6.6	0	0	0	0	0	0	0	0	0	0	1
Dec-02	6,379	1.46	6.4	0	0	0	0	0	0	0	0	0	0	0
Jan-03	5,585	1.51	6.4	1	0	0	0	0	0	0	0	0	0	0
Feb-03	6,032	1.49	6.4	0	1	0	0	0	0	0	0	0	0	0
Mar-03	8,739	1.43	6.3	0	0	1	0	0	0	0	0	0	0	0

Table 8A.2 **Regression results for the full Stoke's Lodge model**

Regression Statistics					
Multiple R	0.923		**DW = 1.883**		
R-square	0.852				
Adjusted R-Square	0.830				
Standard error	743.124				
Observations	101				
ANOVA	*df*	*SS*	*MS*	*F*	*Sig F*
Regression	13	277,032,357	21,310,181	38.589	0.000
Residual	87	48,044,350	552,233.9		
Total	100	325,076,708			
	Coefficients	*Standard error*	*t Stat*	*p-Value*	*p/2*
Intercept	10,270.912	1,065.996	9.635	0.000	0.000
GP	−1,396.275	117.891	−11.844	0.000	0.000
CE	−453.858	162.408	−2.795	0.006	0.003
Jan	547.215	361.715	1.513	0.134	0.067
Feb	1,303.684	361.737	3.604	0.001	0.000
Mar	2,705.610	362.592	7.462	0.000	0.000
Apr	2,140.244	363.438	5.889	0.000	0.000
May	3,671.132	365.245	10.051	0.000	0.000
June	3,650.990	375.260	9.729	0.000	0.000
July	4,305.826	374.846	11.487	0.000	0.000
Aug	4,500.630	375.350	11.990	0.000	0.000
Sept	3,466.594	374.798	9.249	0.000	0.000
Oct	2,550.378	372.192	6.852	0.000	0.000
Nov	547.899	371.616	1.474	0.144	0.072

this model. You may wonder why all the correlations for pairs of monthly dummy variables are not the same. This is because in the data you do not have an equal number of observations for all months. There are five more observations for January through May than for the other seven months.

Table 8A.3 *The correlation matrix for all independent variables. All the correlation Coefficients are Quite Small so multicollinearity is not a problem*

	GP	CE	Jan	Feb	Mar	Apr	May	June	July	Aug	Sept	Oct	Nov
GP	1												
CE	-0.02	1											
Jan	-0.08	0.02	1										
Feb	-0.05	0.02	-0.10	1									
Mar	0.01	0.00	-0.10	-0.10	1								
Apr	0.06	0.01	-0.10	-0.10	-0.10	1							
May	0.13	0.00	-0.10	-0.10	-0.10	-0.10	1						
June	0.02	-0.08	-0.09	-0.09	-0.09	-0.09	-0.09	1					
July	0.01	-0.07	-0.09	-0.09	-0.09	-0.09	-0.09	-0.09	1				
Aug	0.01	-0.08	-0.09	-0.09	-0.09	-0.09	-0.09	-0.09	-0.09	1			
Sept	0.03	-0.06	-0.09	-0.09	-0.09	-0.09	-0.09	-0.09	-0.09	-0.09	1		
Oct	-0.02	0.04	-0.09	-0.09	-0.09	-0.09	-0.09	-0.09	-0.09	-0.09	-0.09	1	
Nov	-0.05	0.10	-0.09	-0.09	-0.09	-0.09	-0.09	-0.09	-0.09	-0.09	-0.09	-0.09	1

The regression equation can be written based on the values in the "Coefficients" column in the regression results shown in Table 8A.2. The equation is:

$$MRO = 10,270.912 - 1,396.275(GP) - 453.858(CE)$$
$$+ 547.215(Jan) + 1,303.684(Feb) + 2705.610(Mar)$$
$$+ 2,140.244(Apr) + 3,671.132(May) + 3,650.990(June)$$
$$+ 4,305.826(July) + 4,500.630(Aug) + 3,466.594(Sept)$$
$$+ 2,550.378(Oct) + 547.899(Nov)$$

Figure 8A.3 shows you how well the predictions from this equation fit the actual occupancy data. You see visually that the fit is quite good. There are some summer peaks that appear to be underestimated. However, overall the fit is good, and certainly better than the fit shown in Figure 8A.2 for which seasonal dummy variables were not included in the model.

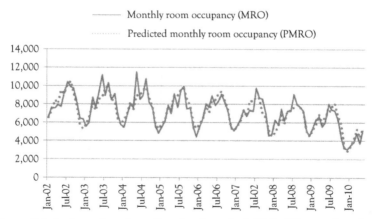

Figure 8A.3 Actual and predicted values for MRO. The predicted values are shown by the dotted line, based on MRO as a function of GP, CE, and 11 seasonal (monthly) dummy variables

CHAPTER 9

Nonlinear Regression Models

Chapter 9 Preview

When you have completed reading this chapter you will be able to:

- Address nonlinearities with linear least squares regression.
- Estimate a nonlinear regression (four different nonlinear regressions).
- Know when it may be reasonable to use a nonlinear regression model.
- Identify common uses of nonlinear regressions.
- Interpret the results from an estimate of a nonlinear model.

Introduction

All of the regression models you have looked at thus far have been linear. Some have had one independent variable, while others have had several independent variables, but all have been linear. Linear functions appear to work very well in many situations. However, cases do arise in which nonlinear models are called for. The real world does not always present you with linear (i.e., straight-line) relationships.

In some situations, the economic/business theory underlying a relationship may lead you to expect a nonlinear relationship. Examples of such real world cases include the U-shaped average cost functions and S-shaped production functions, both of which are caused by the existence of the law of variable proportions or diminishing marginal returns. Profit and revenue functions often increase at a decreasing rate and then decline, shaped somewhat like an inverted-U($\cap$).

Earlier, you learned that plotting data in a scattergram before doing a regression analysis can be helpful. Among other things, this may help us decide on the appropriate form for the model. Perhaps some nonlinear form would appear more consistent with the data than would a linear function.

Quadratic Functions

Look at the two graphs in Figure 9.1. The data for the scattergrams depicted in each graph are listed to the right of the graphs. In the upper graph, the 10 observations appear to form a U-shaped function such as what

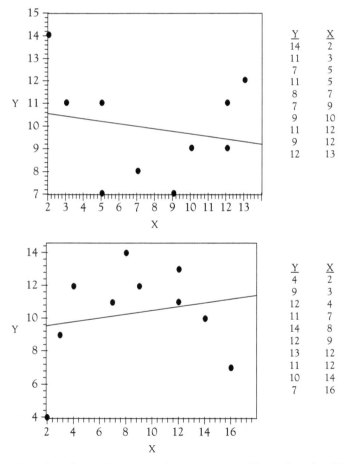

Figure 9.1 *Quadratic functions. Scattergrams of data that should be fit with quadratic functions*

you might expect of an average variable cost curve. The lower scattergram suggests a function that increases at a decreasing rate and then eventually declines (like an upside-down bowl placed on a table). Clearly, a linear function would not fit either set of data very well. This lack of a linear fit is illustrated by the inclusion of the OLS linear regression line in each graph. In neither case does the (linear) regression line offer a close fit for the data.

These scattergrams are indicative of quadratic functions, that is, functions in which X^2 appears as an independent variable. But most regression programs are designed for linear problems. Is it possible to use such programs to estimate this type of function? The answer is "yes" and the technique for doing so is surprisingly simple.

You need only define a new variable to be the square of X. Suppose that you use Z. Then $Z = X^2$. You can now estimate a multiple linear regression model of Y as a function of X and Z, which may be expressed as:

$$Y = a + b_1 X + b_2 Z$$

This is a function that is linear in the variables X and Z.

Estimating a function such as this for the data in the upper graph of Figure 9.1, you get:

$$Y = 18.26 - 2.71X + 0.17Z$$

But remember that $Z = X^2$. Rewriting the function in terms of Y, X, and X^2, you have:

$$Y = 18.26 - 2.71X + 0.17X^2$$

This is a quadratic function in X and has the U-shape you would expect to fit the scattergram (see Figure 9.2).

The data in the lower graph in Figure 9.1 also appear to be quadratic, but this time the function at first goes up and then down (rather than vice versa, as in the previous case). Even though the curvature of this data is an upside-down U-shape, you can use the same technique. Again let $Z = X^2$ and estimate:

$$Y = a + b_1 X + b_2 Z$$

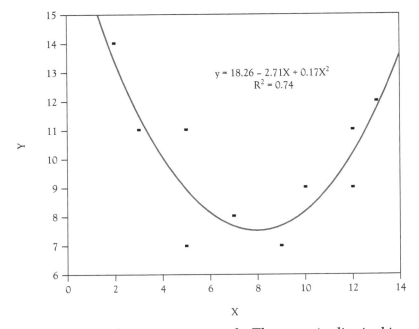

Figure 9.2 A nonlinear regression result. The regression line in this case is nonlinear because a quadratic (squared) term has been added to the regression estimate

This time you expect the sign of b_1 to be positive and the sign of b_2 to be negative (The opposite was true in the previous case). The regression results are:

$$Y = 1.73 + 2.49X - 0.14Z$$

Substituting X^2 for Z, you have:

$$Y = 1.73 + 2.49X - 0.14X^2$$

This function would have the inverted U-shape that the scattergram of the data would suggest (see Figure 9.3).

Cubic Functions

How would you handle situations in which the perceived curve exhibited by a set of data has more than a single curvature? Is OLS regression able

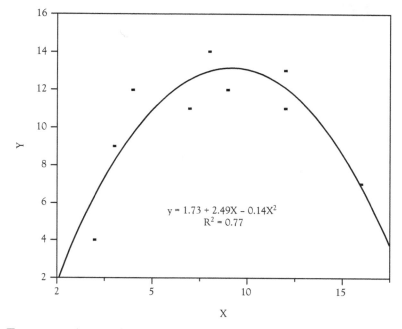

$$y = 1.73 + 2.49X - 0.14X^2$$
$$R^2 = 0.77$$

Figure 9.3 A second nonlinear regression result. The regression line in this case is again nonlinear because a quadratic (squared) term has been added to the regression estimate. However, in this regression, the squared term has a negative coefficient and the resulting regression line is in the form of an upside-down U-shape

to model such data? Yes, you can model data with a double curvature but the technique will require the use of a cubed term. Now take a look at the scattergrams and data shown in Figure 9.4. You can see that a linear function would not fit either of these data sets very well. The data in the upper graph might represent a cost function, while that in the lower graph may be a production function. Both are polynomials, but they are cubic functions, rather than quadratic functions.

To estimate these cubic functions using a multiple linear regression model, you can let $Z = X^2$ and $W = X^3$. The linear function is then:

$$Y = a + b_1X + b_2Z + b_3W$$

Using the data in the lower graph in Figure 9.4, you get the following regression equation:

$$Y = 1.02 + 1.63X - 0.31Z + 0.021W$$

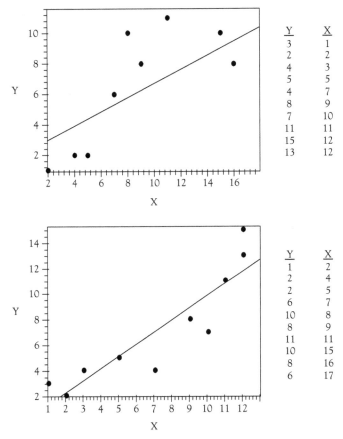

Figure 9.4 Cubic functions. These two data sets should be fit with cubic functions. The OLS linear functions are shown in the scattergrams and are seen to not fit the data well

Substituting X2 for Z and X3 for W, you get:

$$Y = 1.02 + 1.63X - 0.31X^2 + 0.021X^3$$

You can see this result in Figure 9.5.[1]

The *t*-ratios are fairly low even though the function fits the data pretty well which might be puzzling. The main reason is related to the small

---

[1] If you run the regression using the data at the top of Figure 9.4 you get *t*-ratios of 1.15 for X, −1.26 for Z, and 1.80 for W.

$$Y = a + b_1X + b_2Z + b_3W$$

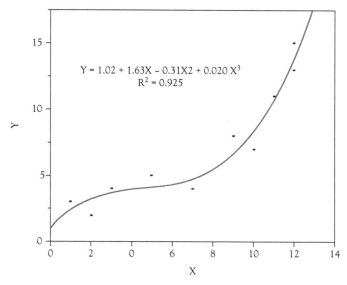

$$Y = 1.02 + 1.63X - 0.31X2 + 0.020 \ X^3$$
$$R^2 = 0.925$$

Figure 9.5 Cubic functions. This cubic form regression is fit with the data from the lower graph in Figure 9.4

number of data points relative to the number of variables. You would rarely estimate a regression analysis with just 10 observations, especially when using 3 independent variables. However, using just 10 observations is helpful in learning the concepts.

You see that the upper scattergram in Figure 9.4 also appears to have two turning points: one near X = 6 and the other in the vicinity of X = 11. This indicates that a cubic function might again be appropriate. You again let $Z = X^2$ and $W = X^3$. The linear function is then:

$$Y = a + b_1X + b_2Z + b_3W$$

Using the data in the upper graph in Figure 9.4, you get the following regression equation:

$$Y = 1.03 - 0.80X + 0.33Z - 0.016W$$

Substituting X^2 for Z and X^3 for W, you get:

$$Y = 1.03 - 0.80X + 0.33X^2 - 0.016X^3$$

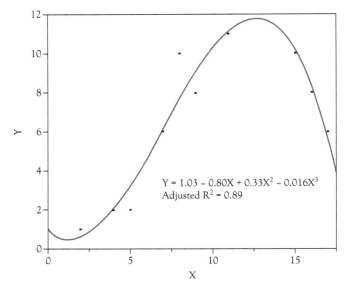

Figure 9.6 Cubic functions. This cubic form regression is fit with the data from the upper graph in Figure 9.4

You can see this result in Figure 9.6.

Reciprocal Functions

Now look at the scattergrams and data in Figure 9.7. In the upper graph, you see that the Y values fall rapidly as X increases at first, but then as X continues to increase, the Y value seems to level off. The lower graph is similar except that, as X increases, at first Y increases rapidly but seems to reach a plateau. Now, consider using a reciprocal transformation to estimate each of these sets of data; that is, use 1/X rather than X as the independent variable.

You can let U = 1/X and proceed to estimate the function: $Y = a + bU$. Using the data from the upper graph in Figure 9.7, the regression equation is:

$$Y = 5.91 + 16.52U$$

Substituting 1/X for U, you have:

$$Y = 5.91 + 16.52(1/X)$$

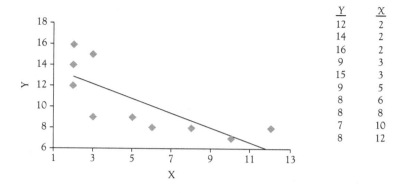

Y	X
12	2
14	2
16	2
9	3
15	3
9	5
8	6
8	8
7	10
8	12

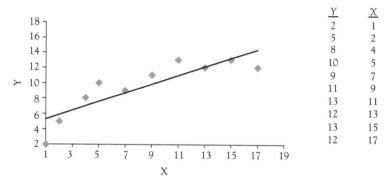

Y	X
2	1
5	2
8	4
10	5
9	7
11	9
13	11
12	13
13	15
12	17

Figure 9.7 Reciprocal functions. The data sets shown here can be fit well with reciprocal functions. The OLS linear functions are shown on each scattergram and are seen to not fit the data well in either case

For this function, as X increases $1/X$ decreases. As a result, this function approaches the value of the constant term of the regression ($a = 5.91$) from above as X gets large as you see in Figure 9.8.

Using the same approach for the data in the lower graph in Figure 9.7, the regression results yield:

$$Y = 12.38 - 11.53(1/X)$$

For this function, as X increases, this function also approaches the value of the constant term of the regression ($a = 12.38$), but from below rather than above. You can see this graphically in Figure 9.9.

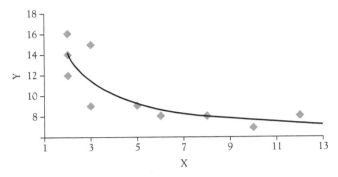

Figure 9.8 *A reciprocal function. This reciprocal form regression is fit with the data from the upper graph in Figure 9.7*

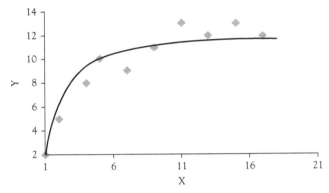

Figure 9.9 *A second reciprocal function. This reciprocal form regression is fit with the data from the lower graph in Figure 9.7*

Multiplicative Functions[2]

The final type of nonlinear function included here involves a double-log transformation. This allows you to use a multiple linear regression program to estimate the following functional form:

$$Y = AX_1{}^{b1}X_2{}^{b2}$$

Functions of this type are called power functions or multiplicative functions. The most common of these functions is the Cobb-Douglas production function. The general form for such a function is:

---

[2] This type of function is often called an "exponential function."

$$Q = AL^{b1}K^{b2}$$

where, Q is output, L is labor input, and K is capital. This example uses just L and K but each of these could have subcomponents so there could be many Ls and many Ks.

These functions are clearly nonlinear, so you must use some transformation to get them into a linear form. If you take the logarithms of both sides of the equation, you have:

$$Y = AX_1^{b1}X_2^{b2}$$
$$\ln Y = \ln A + b_1\ln X_1 + b_2\ln X_2$$

where ln represents the natural logarithm. Now, you can let W = InY, $a = \ln A$, U = lnX1, and $V = \ln X_2$. The function is now linear in W, U, and V, as shown below:

$$W = a + b_1 U + b_2 V$$

A function such as this can be estimated using a standard multiple regression program. For example, consider the data in Table 9.1. Y is the dependent variable, X_1 and X_2 are independent variables, and you would like to estimate the following function:

$$Y = AX_1^{b2}X_2^{b2}$$

Using Excel, you can easily find the natural logarithms of all three variables (W = lnY, U = lnX_1, and $V = \ln X_2$). These values are also shown in Table 9.1.[3]

Using the natural logarithms as the variables, you estimate the following multiple linear regression:

$$W = 2.402 + 0.407U + 0.474V$$

---

[3] Most commercial regression software, including Excel, has this type of transformation function, so you normally never actually see the logarithms of your data.

Table 9.1 Data for a power function

Y	X	X	W = lnY	U = lnX	V = lnX
39.73	1	15	3.682	0.000	2.708
55.37	8	5	4.014	2.079	1.609
41.59	2	9	3.728	0.693	2.197
69.75	6	10	4.245	1.792	2.303
52.25	4	8	3.956	1.386	2.079
87.31	10	11	4.469	2.303	2.398
52.37	5	7	3.958	1.609	1.946
96.60	12	12	4.571	2.485	2.485
66.60	7	8	4.199	1.946	2.079
92.83	9	13	4.531	2.197	2.565

Making the appropriate substitutions for W, U, and V, you have:

$$\ln Y = 2.402 + 0.407 \ln X_1 + 0.474 \ln X_2$$

Taking the antilogarithm of the equation, you obtain:

$$Y = (e^{2.402}) X_1^{.407} X_2^{.474}$$

where e represents the Naperian number (2.7183), which is the base for natural logarithms. Thus,

$$Y = (2.7183^{2.402}) X_1^{.407} X_2^{.474}$$
$$Y = 11.04 X_1^{.407} X_2^{.474}$$

Converting $2.7183^{2.402}$ to 11.04 is easily done using the EXP function in Excel. You see that this fairly complex-looking function can be estimated with relative ease using the power of multiple regression and the logarithmic transformation. Power or multiplicative functions, such as this, are not only commonly found as production functions but are also sometimes used for demand functions.

Even though the basic regression model is designed to estimate linear relationships, nonlinear models can be estimated by using various transformations of the variables. Polynomial functions can be estimated by using second, third, and/or higher powers of one or more of the independent variables. Logarithmic and reciprocal transformations are also commonly used.

What You Have Learned in Chapter 9

- How nonlinearities can be addressed with linear least squares regression.
- To estimate a nonlinear regression (four different nonlinear regressions).
- To recognize when it may be reasonable to use a nonlinear regression model.
- To be familiar with common uses of nonlinear regressions.
- How to interpret the results of an estimate of a nonlinear model.

CHAPTER 10

Abercrombie & Fitch and Jewelry Sales Regression Case Studies[1]

Case I: Abercrombie & Fitch Sales in the United States

The Family Clothing Store industry, in which Abercrombie & Fitch Co. (A&F) operates, is highly fragmented and is dominated by a large number of small retailers, each with a low market share of the total industry. The top four players in this industry are A&F, Gap Inc., American Eagle Outfitters, Inc., and Ross Stores. These four companies collectively account for about 40 percent of the market. A&F generally charges higher prices compared with similar merchandise at Gap and American Eagle. The company was founded in 1892 and is headquartered in New Albany, Ohio.

The Company's stores offer knit and woven shirts, graphic t-shirts, fleece, jeans and woven pants, shorts, sweaters, and outerwear. A&F operates more than one thousand stores in the United States, Canada, and the United Kingdom. It also sells its products through the Internet and catalogues.

The A&F brand targets college students. The RUEHL Brand, launched in 2005 and dropped in 2008, was a mix of business casual and trendy fashion, created to appeal to the modern-minded and post-college customers. In early 2007, the company launched another brand, Gilly Hicks, which specializes in women's underwear, sleepwear, personal care products, and at-home products. This line was dropped at the start of 2014.

---

[1] We thank Laxmi Subhasini Rupesh for background research related to the A&F case.

The Data

To build a regression model for sales of A&F the dependent variable is sales of A&F on a quarterly basis and in thousands of dollars.[2] These values are shown in Figure 10.1 as a time-series plot constructed in Excel. As you see, sales increased from the beginning of this series until the economic downturn in 2008. After the economic downturn sales picked up again until 2013.

You also see sharp peaks that may represent seasonality in their sales. For A&F, the fiscal year runs from February to January, which makes February, March, and April the first quarter and subsequently November, December, and January the last quarter. The data are labeled using the middle month of the quarter. Thus, March represents the first quarter and December represents the fourth quarter of each year.

When you think about constructing a model for a company's sales one of the first things that comes to mind is some measure of consumer buying power. You may know the concept of a "normal good." The products sold by A&F would be considered normal goods. A normal good is one for which sales would increase as income increases. For this example, personal income (PI) in billions of dollars is used as a measure of buying power.

Unemployment often affects retail sales beyond the effect that unemployment has on income. If consumers are unemployed, or if they

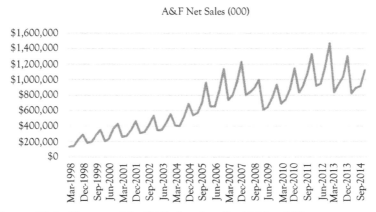

Figure 10.1 Abercrombie & Fitch sales (in 1000s of $)

---

[2] SEC filings at www.sec.gov.

are employed but have concerns about losing their jobs, their purchasing behavior is likely to change. In the case of A&F the clothing and other items they sell would be considered discretionary goods. Thus, in times of high unemployment, consumers may put off purchases from a store such as A&F.

Most retail sales have considerable seasonality. You can see this in Figure 10.1. Therefore, you would want to use dummy variables to evaluate the degree and nature of seasonality.

During the period considered A&F launched two new brands. One was the "RUEHL" brand and the other was "Gilly Hicks." For each brand you could create a dummy variable with a one when that brand existed and zero otherwise. The RUEHL brand was only on the market from 2005 through 2007; so the dummy variable for RUEHL is a one in the 12 quarters covering 2005 through 2007. The other brand, Gilly Hicks, was started in early 2007 and was dropped at the start of 2014. The dummy variable for Gilly Hicks is therefore a one starting in the first quarter of 2007 through the end of 2013, and zero in all other periods.

The Hypotheses

When you do a regression analysis you should think carefully about the expectations you have for each independent variable. Do you expect a positive or negative coefficient for each of the independent variables? For the A&F regression model you have the following potential independent variables: personal income (PI), the unemployment rate (UR), seasonal dummy variables (Q1, Q2, Q3, and Q4), RUEHL brand, and Gilly Hicks brand. Thus, you should think about the direction of the impact each of these could have on A&F sales.

Hypothesis 1. The Expected Influence of Income

When the personal income of individuals increase, they tend to purchase more as their buying power increases. On the other hand, when the personal income falls, their purchasing power is reduced and they lower their purchases of normal goods. Thus, your research hypothesis is that the true regression slope (β) between sales and income should be positive. Thus, your hypotheses for personal income are:

$$H_0 : \beta \leq 0$$
$$H_1 : \beta > 0$$

This form of the statistical test is appropriate for personal income, because you expect a direct relationship between sales of A&F and personal income. You expect an increase (decrease) in personal income to cause an increase (decrease) in A&F sales.

Hypothesis 2. The Expected Influence of the Unemployment Rate

You might expect that there is more than an income effect of unemployment on the sale of consumer goods. You would expect that the sales of A&F would have an inverse relationship with the unemployment rate. Thus, your hypotheses for the unemployment rate are:

$$H_0 : \beta \geq 0$$
$$H_1 : \beta < 0$$

If the unemployment rate increases, then the A&F sales would be expected to decreases and vice versa.

Hypothesis 3. Seasonal Dummy Variables

You might expect that A&F would experience the greatest sales activity during the fall season due to the back-to-school sales as well as in the last part of the year due to holiday gift buying. The first quarter of the year is typically the lowest quarter for retail sales of almost all types of products. Thus, it makes sense to use the first quarter as the base period. As a result, you would expect sales to be higher in quarters two, three, and four than in the first quarter of each year. Thus, your hypotheses for Q2, Q3, and Q4 are all the same as follows:

$$H_0 : \beta \leq 0$$
$$H_1 : \beta > 0$$

Hypothesis 4. RUEHL and Gilly Hicks

With regard to the dummy variables for the RUEHL and the Gilly Hicks brands, you would expect a positive relationship to overall sales. Remember that these two dummy variables are equal to 1 when the brand exists and equal to 0 when the brand does not exist. Thus the hypotheses for each of these brands (RUEHL and Gilly Hicks) would be:

$$H_0 : \beta \leq 0$$
$$H_1 : \beta > 0$$

The Regression Models

To help you see the development of regression models, four models of A&F sales are discussed in this section. The first includes only one independent variable (personal income), the second adds unemployment, the third also includes seasonal dummy variables, and finally, the fourth model adds the two dummy variables related to the RUEHL and Gilly Hicks brands.

For each model you will see the Excel regression results and a graph of the actual A&F sales compared with the predictions from each model. You will also see a brief discussion of the five-step evaluation of each model. We do not show the ANOVA for each of the four models since the F-ratios are significant for all four at a 95 percent confidence level.

Model 1. Sales as a Function of Personal Income

First, look at the regression results from Excel in Table 10.1. As you see, the Excel regression output has been edited to help you concentrate on the most important parts of the tables. These results will form the basis for your five-step evaluation of the first model.

The most important statistical results are in bold in the Excel output in Table 10.1. From the *Coefficients* column you can write the equation for this model as:

$$\text{Sales} = -729{,}607.4 + 144.340 \ (\text{PI})$$

Table 10.1 A&F sales as a function of personal income

S = f(PI)				
Regression Statistics				
R-square	0.789		DW = 1.656	
Adjusted R-square	0.786			
Standard error	153,886			
Observations	68			
	Coefficients	*t Stat*	*P-Value*	*P/2*
Intercept	−729,607.4	15.7085.7087.773	0.000	0.000
PI	144.340	9.189	0.000	0.000

Step 1: Is the Model Logical?

You would expect that as consumers' incomes increase A&F would sell more goods. Therefore, the positive (+) sign for the coefficient (slope) related to income is logical.

Step 2: Is the Slope Term Significantly Positive?

In order to check for statistical significance of the independent variable (PI) the hypothesis for the slope of income is subjected to a one-tailed t-test. If the absolute value of calculated tc is greater than the t-table value at the 95 percent confidence level (5 percent significance level), you can reject the null hypothesis. This means that you have empirical support for the research hypothesis. To determine the t-table value, the degree of freedom (df) is calculated as $df = n - (k + 1)$. In this case, n = number of observations in the model = 68 and k = number of independent variables = 1. Thus, $df = 68 - (1 + 1) = 66$. The t-table value is approximately 1.671 (see Appendix 4B, and use the row for df=60, which is the closest value to 66).

The calculated t-ratio for disposable personal income is 9.189. This would be very far into the right tail of the distribution as indicated by a *P-value* of 0 to three decimal places. In the Excel output table, you see a column that is added for the p-value divided by two (*P/2*) because you would be doing a one-tailed test and the *P*-value provided by Excel is for both tails of the distribution. Of course, *P/2* is also less than the desired level of significance of 0.05. Thus, there is very little risk of error in rejecting the null hypothesis.

Step 3: What is the Explanatory Power of the Model?

For this bivariate regression model, the explanatory power is measured by the coefficient of determination, R^2. The coefficient of determination tells you the percentage of the variation in the dependent variable (A&F sales) that is explained by the one independent variable, personal income (PI). In this model, the coefficient of determination (R^2) is 0.789, which means 78.9 percent of the variation in the A&F sales is explained by this model.

Step 4: Check for Serial Correlation

Because time-series data are used in this model you need to be concerned about possible serial correlation. You can evaluate this using the DW statistic. The DW statistic will always be in the range of 0–4 and as a rule of thumb, a value between 1.5 and 2.5 is suggestive that there may be no serial correlation.

The DW statistic for this model is 1.656. Based on the table in Appendix 4C and the discussion in Appendix 4D you see that du $< 1.656 < 2$, so Test 4 is satisfied and you can say that no serial correlation exists. For this case, you would use du $= 1.544$ with $n = 40$ and $k = 1$.[3]

Step 5: Check for Multicollinearity

For a simple model with only one independent variable there is no possible multicollinearity. In Figure 10.2, the graph shows the actual A&F sales (solid line) along with the predictions based on Model 1 (dotted line). What do you think is most clearly missing in the model?

Model 2. Sales as a Function of Personal Income and Unemployment Rate

Now we will expand Model 1 to include more variables in Models 2 through 4. Your evaluation of each model should follow the same format

---

[3] You would use 40 rather than $n = 68$ because the table only goes as high as 40.

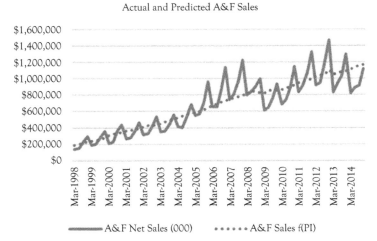

Figure 10.2 A&F actual sales (solid line) and predictions (dotted line) based on Model 1

as for Model 1. Looking at three more models of sales for A&F will help you understand how models are developed and evaluated.

Suppose that next you decide to add the unemployment rate as an additional independent variable. Again you should first look at the regression results from Excel shown in Table 10.2. Here PI = personal income and UR = unemployment rate.

The Excel results in Table 10.2 provide the basis for your five-step evaluation of the second model. The most important statistical results are in bold. From the *Coefficients* column you can write the equation for this model as:

$$\text{Sales} = -724{,}899.5 + 156.675 \, (\text{PI}) - 20{,}386.882 \, (\text{UR})$$

Step 1: Is the Model Logical?

Again, you expect that as consumers' incomes increase A&F would sell more goods so the positive (+) sign for the slope related to income is logical. And, you would expect that a higher unemployment would result in lower sales. Thus, the negative slope for UR is logical.

Step 2: Are the Slope Terms Significantly Positive?

Now you need to evaluate each of the two slope terms. Since you now have two independent variables df = $n - (k + 1) = 68 - (2 + 1) = 65$. Because

Table 10.2 A&F sales as a function of personal income and the unemployment rate

S = f(PI,UR)				
Regression Statistics				
R-square	0.796		DW = 1.708	
Adjusted R-square	0.789			
Standard error	152,550			
Observations	68			
	Coefficients	*t Stat*	*P-Value*	*P/2*
Intercept	−724,899.5	−7.983	0.000	0.000
PI	156.675	12.651	0.000	0.000
UR	−20,386.882	−1.470	0.146	0.073

the closest value for df in your table is 60, you would again use a *t*-table value of 1.671. For personal income, the calculated *t*-statistics is well into the upper tail of the distribution. However, for the unemployment rate the calculated t is not out in the lower tail of the distribution. Further, only for income (PI) is *P*/2 is less than the level of significance of 0.05. This means that you have empirical support that income has a significant influence on A&E sales at a 95 percent confidence level. However, the *P*/2 value for the unemployment rate exceeds the 0.05 critical value so we cannot say the same for UR. We can say that unemployment has a significant affect on sales if we lower our confidence level to 90 percent, which is not uncommon (note that *P*/2 for UR is less than 0.10).

Step 3: What is the Explanatory Power of the Model?

For this multiple regression model, the explanatory power is measured by the coefficient of determination, but now you must use the adjusted R-square. This coefficient of determination tells you the percentage of the variation in the dependent variable (A&F sales) that is explained by PI and the UR. In this model, the coefficient of determination (adjusted R^2) is 0.789, which means 78.9 percent of the variation in the A&F sales is explained by this model. This is essentially the same as for the bivariate model. The R-square is higher for this model but because we have lost one degree of freedom it turns out that the adjusted R-square is the same as the R-square for the bivariate model.

Step 4: Check for Serial Correlation

Again you need to be concerned about possible serial correlation. The DW statistic for this model is 1.708. Based on the table in Appendix 4C and the discussion in Appendix 4D you see that $1.600 < 1.708 < 2$, so Test 4 is satisfied and you can say that no serial correlation exists. For this case, you would use du $= 1.600$ with $n = 40$ (rather than $n = 68$) and $k = 2$.

Step 5: Check for Multicollinearity

With more than one independent variable you need to look at the correlation matrix for all pairs of independent variables. The correlation between PI and UR is 0.68, so the two variables are not strongly enough correlated to cause a problem. Also, there is no indication in the model of a multicollinearity problem, since both signs for coefficients are as you expect.

In Figure 10.3, you see a graph that shows the actual A&F sales (solid line) along with the predictions based on Model 2 (dotted line). This model fits a bit better than Model 1 but it is not as good as you would hope. What do you think is still missing?

Model 3. Sales as a Function of PI, UR, and Two Seasonal Dummy Variables (Q3 and Q4)

Having recognized that both Models 1 and 2 failed to account for the seasonal variation in A&F sales, you would naturally try to add seasonal

Figure 10.3 A&F actual sales (solid line) and predictions (dotted line) based on Model 2

dummy variables. Analysis of the data shows that there is only significant seasonality during the back to school and holiday seasons (quarters Q3 and Q4). Therefore, you only need seasonal dummy variables for these two quarters of each year.

You rely upon the regression results from Excel as shown in Table 10.3 to evaluate Model 3. Here PI = personal income, and UR = the unemployment rate, while Q3 and Q4 represent the corresponding quarters. From the *Coefficients* column, you can write the equation for this model as:

$$\text{Sales} = -794{,}137.7 + 152.208 \,(\text{PI}) - 1t7{,}766.012 \,(\text{UR}) \\ + 110{,}692.074 \,(\text{Q3}) + 276{,}248.649 \,(\text{Q4})$$

Step 1: Is the Model Logical?

Again, you expect that as consumers' incomes increase A&F would sell more goods and as unemployment increases they would be expected to sell less. Thus, a positive sign for the slope related to income is logical as is the negative sign for unemployment. You would expect quarters Q3 and Q4 to have higher sales than the rest of the year due to back to school and holiday shopping. Q3 is a dummy variable equal to 1 every third

Table 10.3 A&F sales as a function of personal income, the unemployment rate, and seasonal dummy variables for Q3 and Q4

S = f(PI,UR,Q3,Q4)				
Regression Statistics				
R-square	0.913		DW = 0.737	
Adjusted R-square	0.907			
Standard error	101,302			
Observations	68			
	Coefficients	*t Stat*	*P-Value*	*P/2*
Intercept	−794,137.7	−13.012	0.000	0.000
PI	152.208	18.474	0.000	0.000
UR	−17,766.012	−1.928	0.058	0.029
Q3(Aug–Oct)	110,692.074	3.676	0.000	0.000
Q4(Nov–Jan)	276,248.649	9.164	0.000	0.000

quarter and 0 otherwise. Q4 is a dummy variable equal to 1 every fourth quarter and 0 otherwise. Thus, the positive coefficients for Q3 and Q4 make sense.

Step 2: Are the Slope Terms Significantly Positive?

Now you need to evaluate all four slope terms. Since you now have four independent variables, df $= n - (k + 1) = 68 - (4 + 1) = 63$. Again you would use a t-table value of 1.671. For all four variables, the calculated t-statistics are well into the tails of the distribution (the upper tail for PI, Q3, Q4, and the lower tail for UR). Further, in all cases $P/2$ is less than the desired level of significance of 0.05. This means that you have empirical support for all four of the research hypotheses (at greater than a 95 percent confidence level).

Step 3: What is the Explanatory Power of the Model?

For this multiple regression model, the explanatory power is again measured by the adjusted R-square. This value tells you the percentage of the variation in the dependent variable (A&F sales) that is explained by PI, UR, and seasonality as measured by Q3 and Q4. In this model, the adjusted R-square is 0.907, which means 90.7 percent of the variation in the A&F sales is explained by this model. This is a big improvement and helps you to see the importance of seasonality as measured by using dummy variables for seasonality.

Step 4: Check for Serial Correlation

Again you need to be concerned about possible serial correlation. The DW statistic for this model is 0.737. Based on the table in Appendix 4C and the discussion in Appendix 4D, you see that $0 < 0.737 < d_1 = 1.285$ so Test 6 is satisfied, which means that this model has a positive serial correlation problem. This means that standard errors may be underestimated and thus t-ratios may be larger than they should be and some null hypotheses may have been incorrectly rejected in favor of the research hypotheses. Given the sizes of the t-ratios calculated, this is most likely to be a problem related to unemployment rather than the other independent variables, since the other t-ratios are very large. One solution may be that you are missing some useful causal (independent) variables.

Step 5: Check for Multicollinearity

With more than one independent variable, you need to look at the correlation matrix for all pairs of independent variables. The correlation matrix is shown in Table 10.4. The correlations between the individual pairs of independent variables in this model are not very high as shown in the correlation matrix in Table 10.4. Also, there is no indication in the model of a multicollinearity problem, since the signs for all four coefficients are as you expect.

In Figure 10.4, you see a graph that shows the actual A&F sales (solid line) along with the predictions based on Model 3 (dotted line). This model fits much better than Model 2 but has a positive serial correlation issue.

Model 4. Sales as a Function of Personal Income, Unemployment Rate, Two Seasonal Dummy Variables (Q3 and Q4), and Dummy Variables for Two Brands

During the period for which data have been used, A&F added the RUEHL brand in 2005 then dropped it in 2008. They added the Gilly Hicks brand in 2007, but dropped that brand in 2014. For each quarter in the data, the RUEHL and the Gilly Hicks brands either were or were not part of A&F. Thus, you can create a dummy variable for each brand that equals 1 when the brand was active and 0 otherwise.

Let us now look at one more regression model. In this last model we will include PI, UR, Q3, Q4, the RUEHL brand, and the Gilly Hicks brand as independent variables.

Table 10.4 Correlation matrix for personal income (PI), the unemployment rate (UR), and seasonal dummy variables for Q3 and Q4

	PI	UR	Q3(Aug–Oct)	Q4(Nov–Jan)
PI	1.000			
UR	0.68	1.000		
Q3(Aug–Oct)	0.02	0.01	1.000	
Q4(Nov–Jan)	0.04	0.01	−0.33	1.000

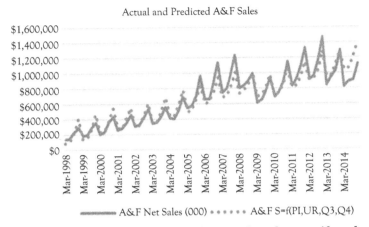

Figure 10.4 A&F actual sales (solid line) and predictions (dotted line) based on Model 3

These results, as shown in Table 10.5, form the basis for your Five-step evaluation of the fourth (and last) model. From the *Coefficients* column you can write this equation as:

$$Sales = -641{,}007.4 + 125.007 \ (PI) - 13{,}720.666 \ (UR)$$
$$+ 114{,}806.255 \ (Q3) + 282{,}904.094 \ (Q4)$$
$$+ 147{,}302.158 \ (R) + 142{,}508.792 \ (GH)$$

Step 1: Is the Model Logical?

Again, you expect that A&F would sell more goods as PI increases, when it is a third or fourth quarter and when they have the RUEHL and Gilly Hicks brands. You would expect them to have lower sales if unemployment increases. Therefore, all six slope terms in the model have signs for their coefficients that make sense.

Step 2: Are the Slope Terms Significantly Positive?

Now you need to evaluate all six slope terms. Now that you have six independent variables, df $= n - (k + 1) = 68 - (6 + 1) = 61$. Again you would use a t-table value of 1.671. For five of the six independent variables the calculated t-statistics are well into the tails of the distribution

Table 10.5 *A&F sales as a function of personal income, the*
unemployment rate, seasonal dummy variables for Q3 and Q4, and
dummy variables for the RUEHL and Gilly Hicks brands

S = f(PI,UR,Q3,Q4,R,GH)				
Regression Statistics				
R-square	0.958		DW = 1.492	
Adjusted R-square	0.954			
Standard error	71,332			
Observations	68			
	Coefficients	*t Stat*	*p-Value*	*P/2*
Intercept	−641,007.4	−11.544	0.000	0.000
PI	125.007	18.644	0.000	0.000
UR	−13,720.666	−1.642	0.106	0.053
Q3(Aug–Oct)	114,806.255	5.413	0.000	0.000
Q4(Nov–Jan)	282,904.094	13.316	0.000	0.000
RUEHL Brand	147,302.158	5.586	0.000	0.000
Gilly Hicks Brand	142,508.792	5.174	0.000	0.000

(the upper tail for PI, Q3, Q4, RUEHL, and Gilly Hicks). For the unemployment rate (UR), the calculated t-ratio of -1.642 is slightly less negative than the t-table value of -1.671. Certainly all six independent variables would have a significant impact on A&F sales at a 90 percent confidence level, which is also commonly used. It is likely that an analyst would leave all six of the current independent variables in the model. This is especially true since the $P/2$ value for unemployment is 0.053.

This means that there is strong statistical support for the positive influence of personal income, quarter 3, quarter 4, the RUEHL brand and the Gilly Hicks brand on sales revenue for A&E. There is some support for a negative affect of the unemployment rate on sales, but the statistical support is not as strong as for the other causal variables.

Step 3: What is the Explanatory Power of the Model?

For this multiple regression model, the explanatory power is again measured by the adjusted R^2. In this model the adjusted R^2 is 0.954, which means 95.4 percent of the variation in the A&F sales is explained by PI, UR, seasonality, and the existence of the RUEHL and Gilly Hicks brands. This is an improvement over Model 3.

Step 4: Check for Serial Correlation

Again you need to be concerned about possible serial correlation. The DW statistic for this model is 1.492. Based on the table in Appendix 4C and the discussion in Appendix 4D you see that $d_l = 1.175 < 1.492 < d_u = 1.854$ ($n = 40$ and $k = 6$).

Test 3 is satisfied This means that the test for serial correlation is indeterminate.[4] By adding two additional variables that have a significant effect on A&F sales has alleviated the potential serial correlation that you observed in Model 3.

Step 5: Check for Multicollinearity

You know that with more than one independent variable you need to look at the correlation matrix for all pairs of independent variables. The correlations between the individual pairs of independent variables in this model are not very high as shown by the correlation matrix below in Table 10.6. Also, there is no indication in the model of a multicollinearity problem, since the signs for all four coefficients are as you expect.

Table 10.6 Correlation matrix for personal income (PI), the unemployment rate(UR), seasonal dummy variables for Q3 and Q4, and dummy variables for RUEHL and Gilly Hicks

	PI	UR	Q3 (Aug–Oct)	Q4 (Nov–Jan)	RUEHL brand	Gilly Hicks brand
PI	1.00					
UR	0.68	1.00				
Q3 (Aug–Oct)	0.02	0.01	1.00			
Q4 (Nov–Jan)	0.04	0.01	−0.33	1.00		
RUEHL brand	0.03	−0.35	0.00	0.00	1.00	
Gilly Hicks brand	0.69	0.71	0.00	0.00	−0.07	1.00

---

[4] For this case, you would use $d_l = 1.175$ and $d_u = 1.854$.

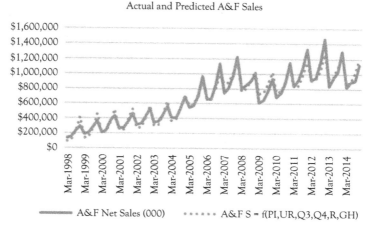

Figure 10.5 shows Actual and Predicted A&F Sales with axis labels from $0 to $1,600,000 and dates from Mar-1998 through Mar-2014. Legend: A&F Net Sales (000) and A&F S = f(PI,UR,Q3,Q4,R,GH)

Figure 10.5 *A&F actual sales (solid line) and predictions (dotted line) based on Model 4*

In Figure 10.5, you see a graph that shows the actual A&F sales (solid line) along with the predictions based on Model 4 (dotted line). This model fits very well and does not have a positive serial correlation problem.

Case II: Retail Jewelry Sales in the United States

This case involves the total sales of jewelry stores in the United States (U.S. Retail Sales: Jewelry Stores. NAICS 44831, in millions of dollars. Source: economagic.com). The original data were on a monthly basis, however to simplify the number of dummy variables needed to deal with seasonality the data have been transformed to a quarterly basis. See Figure 10.6.

In Figure 10.6 you see that jewelry sales have generally been increasing over the period used for this example (the first quarter of 2004 through the last quarter of 2014). There was a drop during 2008 when the U.S. economy had a general downturn that affected most economic activity.

Model 1. Jewelry Sales as a Function of Disposable Personal Income Per Capita

We will build a series of regression models to help you see how one can evaluate models working toward a model that is appropriate for the

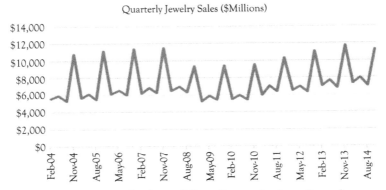

**Figure 10.6 U.S. Jewelry Store Sales. Quarterly data show the
seasonality and trend in jewelry sales**

analyst's use. For a product such as jewelry sales one of the first variables
one might think of is a measure of consumer buying power. For this
purpose we have selected disposable personal income per capita (DPIPC).
This measure of income is the average amount people earn in one year in
the United States.

As we look at several models for jewelry sales we will go through the
five step evaluation process that you have seen in previous examples. The
regression results for the first model of jewelry sales (JS) as a function of
disposable personal income per capita (DPIPC) are shown in Table 10.7.

Look at the regression results from Excel in Table 10.7. The Excel
regression output has been edited to help you concentrate on the most
important parts of the table which are in bold. From the *Coefficients*
column you can write the equation for this model as:

$$JS = 1,333.545 + 0.169 \text{ (DPIPC)}$$

Step 1: Is the Model Logical?

One would expect that jewelry sales would be positively related to how
much money people have to spend. Therefore, the positive sign of the
slope for DPIPC makes sense from an economic/business perspective.

The dotted regression line in Figure 10.7 follows the general upward
trend in jewelry sales but has two things that you will recognize as being
not quite what one might expect. First, the model fails to account for the

Table 10.7 Jewelry sales (JS) as a function of purchasing power as measured by disposable personal income per capita (DPIPC)

Regression Statistics					
R Square	0.065		DW = 2.637		
Standard Error	2007.228				
Observations	44				
	Coefficients	*Standard Error*	*t Stat*	*P-value*	*P/2*
Intercept	1333.545	3560.528	0.375	0.710	0.355
DPIPC	0.169	0.098	1.711	0.094	0.047

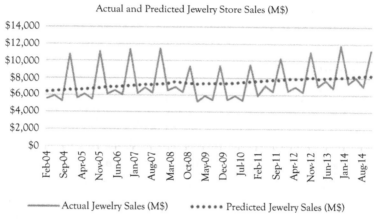

Actual and Predicted Jewelry Store Sales (M$)

━━━ Actual Jewelry Sales (M$)   • • • • • Predicted Jewelry Sales (M$)

Figure 10.7 Jewelry sales as a function of disposable personal income per capita. The solid line represents actual sales while the dotted line is for the predicted values

seasonality in the data. We know this can be helped by using seasonal dummy variables which we will do shortly. Also, notice that during the economic downturn of 2008 the regression line does not seem to drop off as much as one might expect. We will address this in our second model. First, let us continue with the evaluation of the current regression model (JS = f(DPIPC)).

Step 2: Is the Slope Term Significantly Positive?

In order to check for statistical significance of the independent variable (DPIPC) the hypothesis for the slope of income is subjected to a one-tailed *t*-test. If the absolute value of calculated t_c is greater than the *t*-table value at the 95 percent confidence level (5 percent significance level), you can reject the null hypothesis that the relation between JS and DPIPC is not positive.

$$H_0 : \beta \leq 0$$
$$H_1 : \beta > 0$$

This would mean that you have empirical support for the research hypothesis that there is a positive relation between JS and DPIPC.

To determine the *t*-table value, the degree of freedom (df) is calculated as df = $n - (k + 1)$. In this case, n = number of observations in the model = 44 and k = number of independent variables = 1. Thus, df = 44 – (1 + 1) = 42. The *t*-table value is approximately 1.684 (see Appendix 4B, and use the row for df = 40, which is the closest value to 42).

The calculated *t*-ratio for disposable personal income is 1.711. Would this would be in the right tail of the distribution? The answer is "Yes" because 1.711 is greater than 1.684. We see that the *p-value* is 0.094, which is greater than 0.05 – our desired significance level. However, the default t- statistic in Excel output is for a two tailed test. Thus, we need to divide that value by two since we are doing a one tailed test.

In the Excel output table, you see a column for the *p*-value divided by two (*p/2*). Here, *p-value/2* is 0.047 and is less than the desired level of significance of 0.05. Thus, there we can reject the null hypothesis and conclude that we have evidence of a positive relationship between jewelry sales (JS) and income (DPIPC).

Step 3: What is the Explanatory Power of the Model?

For this bivariate regression model, the explanatory power is measured by the coefficient of determination, R^2. In this model, the coefficient of determination (R^2) is 0.065, which means 6.5 percent of the variation in the JS sales is explained by DPIPC. This may seem a small amount of explanatory power, but keep in mind we have just one independent variable at this point and we have not yet dealt with the pronounced seasonality in JS.

Step 4: Check for Serial Correlation

Because time-series data are used in this model you need to be concerned about possible serial correlation. The DW statistic for this model is 2.637. For this case, you would use $d_l = 1.442$ and $d_u = 1.544$ with $n = 40$ and $k = 1$. Based on the table in Appendix 4C and the discussion in Appendix 4D you see that $4 - d_l < 2.637 < 4$, so Test 1 is satisfied and therefore this model has negative serial correlation. For now we will not worry about this result but it does signal to us to watch for serial correlation as we continue to develop the model.

Step 5: Check for Multicollinearity

For a simple model with only one independent variable there is no possible multicollinearity.

Model 2. Jewelry Sales as a Function of Disposable Personal Income Per Capita (DPIPC) and the Unemployment Rate (UR).

In Figure 10.7 we saw that when the only independent variable was DPIPC the regression predictions did not seem to account very well for the economic downturn in 2008. This suggests that we might want to include another variable that might account for a different dimension of the economic slump. We will consider the unemployment rate (UR) in this regard. So we will now have the following model:

$$JS = f (DPIPC, UR)$$

The statistical results for this model are in Table 10.8.

Step 1: Is the Model Logical?

One would still expect that jewelry sales would be positively related to how much money people have to spend. Therefore, the positive sign of the slope for DPIPC makes sense from an economic/business perspective. For the unemployment rate we might expect a negative relationship to

Table 10.8 Jewelry sales (JS) as a function of disposable personal income per capita (DPIPC) and the unemployment Rate (UR)

Regression Statistics					
R Square	0.127		DW = 2.816		
Adjusted R Square	0.084				
Standard Error	1963.186				
Observations	44				
	Coefficients	Standard Error	t Stat	P-value	p/2
Intercept	441.836	3521.477	0.125	0.901	0.450
DPIPC	0.251	0.108	2.330	0.025	0.012
UR	−306.763	179.964	−1.705	0.096	0.048

jewelry sales because jewelry sales are generally something that could be delayed when consumers are worried about their employment situations. Thus, the negative coefficient for UR is logical. The regression equation is:

$$JS = 441.836 + 0.251 \ (DPIPC) - 306.763 \ (UR).$$

The actual JS data and the regression line for Model 2 are graphed in Figure 10.8. The dotted regression line in Figure 10.8 follows the downturn in sales better than the results from Model 1 had done.

Step 2: Are the Slope Terms Significantly Positive or Negative?

Once more the hypothesis for DPIPC is:

$$H_0 : \beta \leq 0$$
$$H_1 : \beta > 0$$

For the unemployment rate the hypothesis is:

$$H_0 : \beta \geq 0$$
$$H_1 : \beta < 0$$

This is because our research hypothesis is that there would be a negative relationship between JS and UR.

To determine the t-table value, the degree of freedom (df) is still calculated as df $= n - (k + 1)$. In this case, $n = 44$ and $k = 2$. Thus, df $= 44 - (1 + 2) = 41$. The t-table value is approximately 1.684 (see Appendix 4B, and use the row for df $= 40$, which is the closest value to 41).

The calculated t-ratio for disposable personal income is 2.330. This would be in the right tail of the distribution as indicated by a *P-value* of 0.025, and $P/2$ of 0.012. Notice that when UR is added to the model the t-statistic for DPIPC is higher than when only DPIPC is in the model. We see that the risk of error in rejecting the null hypothesis for DPIPC is low.

The calculated t-ratio for the unemployment rate is -1.705 which is more negative than the table value of -1.684. Correspondingly, you see that $P/2$ is 0.048 which is less than 0.05. Thus, we have empirical support that there is a negative relation between JS and UR.

Step 3: What is the Explanatory Power of the Model?

For this multiple regression model, the explanatory power is measured by the coefficient of determination, now the adjusted R^2. In this model, the adjusted R^2 is 0.084, which means 8.4 percent of the variation in the JS sales is explained by DPIPC. This may still seem a small amount of explanatory power, but it is more than when only income was considered. Keep in mind we not yet dealt with the pronounced seasonality in JS.

Step 4: Check for Serial Correlation

The DW statistic for this model is 2.816. For this case, you would use $d_l = 1.391$ and $d_u = 1.600$ with $n = 40$ and $k = 2$. Based on the table in Appendix 4C and the discussion in Appendix 4D you see that $4 - d_l < 2.816 < 4$, so Test 1 is again satisfied and therefore this model also has negative serial correlation.

Step 5: Check for Multicollinearity

For a multiple regression model we need to consider whether or not there may be multicollinearity. To check for this we look at the bivariate correlations between all pairs of independent variables. This is shown in

Table 10.9 Correlation matrix for all independent
variables considered in creating a model for jewelry sales

	DPIPC	UR	Q2	Q4
DPIPC	1.00			
UR	0.45	1.00		
Q2	−0.01	0.00	1.00	
Q4	0.07	0.00	−0.33	1.00

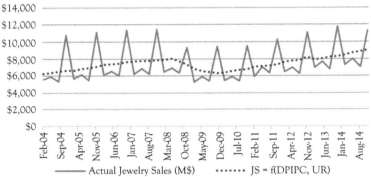

Figure 10.8 Jewelry sales as a function of disposable personal income per capita and the unemployment rate. The solid line represents actual sales while the dotted line is for the predicted values

Table 10.9. We see that the correlation between income (DPIPC) and the unemployment rate (UR) is only 0.45 which is not high enough to suggest a great degree of overlap between the two variables.

The regression model for JS = f (DPIPC and UR) is shown in Figure 10.8. In this figure you see that by adding the unemployment rate the economic downturn in 2008 is more evident in the predicted values (the dotted line). What is missing is the seasonality in the actual jewelry sales.

Model 3. Jewelry Sales as a Function of Disposable Personal Income Per Capita (DPIPC), the Unemployment Rate (UR) and Seasonal Dummy Variables

In Figures 10.7 and 10.8 we saw that the two models used so far do not account for the seasonality in the jewelry sales data. This suggests that we might want to include dummy variables to account for the seasonality in the data. We know that we cannot use dummy variables for all four quarters. The most that we can use is three (one less than the number of possibilities for the seasonal aspect that we are trying to model).

We took the base model with jewelry sales as a function of DPIPC and UR and added dummy variables for quarters one, two, and three. The coefficients for the dummy variables representing all three quarters were negative which told us that quarter four was the highest quarter for jewelry sales. This was not a surprise since during the holiday season many people give jewelry as a gift. The quarter with the most negative coefficient was quarter three, indicating that Q3 is the lowest quarter for sales. We replaced Q3 with Q1 and found that the coefficient for Q1 had a P-value of about 0.30, indicating that Q1 is not significantly different than Q3. This told us that only Q2 and Q4 had significant seasonality.

Now we want a model with DPIPC, UR, Q2, and Q4. So we will now have the following model:

$$JS = f (DPIPC, UR, Q2, Q4).$$

The statistical results for this model are in Table 10.10.

Table 10.10 *Jewelry sales (JS) as a function of disposable personal income per capita (DPIPC), the unemployment Rate (UR), and two dummy variables to account for seasonality*

Jewelry sales = (DPIPC, UR, Q2, Q3)				
Regression Statistics				
R Square	0.965		DW = 1.677	
Adjusted R Square	0.962			
Standard Error	400.765			
Observations	44			
	Coefficients	*t Stat*	*P-value*	*P/2*
Intercept	956.111	1.328	0.192	0.096
DPIPC	0.194	8.756	0.000	0.000
UR	−262.435	−7.138	0.000	0.000
Q2	599.312	4.049	0.000	0.000
Q4	4,467.020	30.074	0.000	0.000

Step 1: Is the Model Logical?

One would still expect that jewelry sales would be positively related to how much money people have to spend. Therefore, the positive sign of the slope for DPIPC makes sense from an economic/business perspective. For the unemployment rate we might expect a negative relationship to jewelry sales because jewelry sales are generally something that could be delayed when consumers are worried about their employment situations. Thus, the negative coefficient for UR is logical. The positive coefficients for Q2 and Q4 are logical since the model is based on the lowest quarters of the year.

The regression equation is:

$$JS = 956.111 + 0.194(DPIPC) - 262.435(UR) + 599.312(Q2) \\ + 4{,}467.020(Q4).$$

The actual JS data and the regression line for Model 3 are graphed in Figure 10.9. The dotted regression line in Figure 10.9 follows the actual values much better than either of the previous models.

Step 2: Are the Slope Terms Significantly Positive or Negative?

Once more the hypothesis for DPIPC is:

$$H_0 : \beta \le 0$$
$$H_1 : \beta > 0.$$

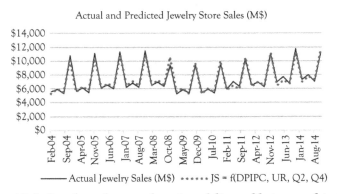

Figure 10.9 Jewelry sales as a function of disposable personal income per capita, the unemployment rate, and dummy variables for quarters two and four (Q2 and Q4). The solid line represents actual sales while the dotted line is for the predicted values

And, for the unemployment rate the hypothesis is:

$$H_0 : \beta \geq 0$$
$$H_1 : \beta < 0.$$

For Q2 and Q3 the hypotheses would be:

$$H_0 : \beta \leq 0$$
$$H_1 : \beta > 0.$$

Because the model is based on the lowest part of the year we expect the coefficients for other quarters to be positive.

To determine the t-table value, the degree of freedom (df) is still calculated as $df = n - (k + 1)$. We know that $n = 44$ and now $k = 4$. Thus, $df = 44 - (1 + 4) = 39$. Again the t-table value is approximately 1.684 (see Appendix 4B, and use the row for $df = 40$, which is the closest value to 39).

The calculated t-ratio for disposable personal income is 8.756. This would far into the right tail of the distribution as indicated by a *P-value* of 0.000, and *P*/2 of 0.000. Notice that in this model the t-statistic for DPIPC is higher than either of the first two models. We see that the risk of error in rejecting the null hypothesis for DPIPC is low.

The calculated t-ratio for the unemployment rate is −7.138 which is more negative than the table value of −1.684. Again note that now that seasonality is accounted for the unemployment rate has a much higher t-statistic. Here both the P-value and *P*/2 are 0.000, which is far is less than 0.05.

For Q2 and Q4 the t-ratios are very large and positive. Thus, we have empirical support that there is a positive relationship between jewelry sales and quarters 2 and 4. The fourth quarter is high due to holiday gift giving. But, what about quarter 2? This quarter includes April, May, and June. These months include Mother's Day, Father's Day, many school graduations and many weddings. All of these can be occasions for which new jewelry might be purchased either for one's self or as gifts.

Step 3: What is the Explanatory Power of the Model?

For this multiple regression model, the explanatory power is measured by the coefficient of determination, now the adjusted R^2. In this model, the adjusted R^2 is 0.962, which means 96.2 percent of the variation in jewelry store sales is explained by DPIPC, UR, Q2, and Q4. Now that seasonality is included the model is a great deal better than the first two models in terms of the explanatory power of the model.

Step 4: Check for Serial Correlation

The DW statistic for this model is 1.677. For this case, you would use $d_l = 1.285$ and $d_u = 1.721$ with $n = 40$ and $k = 4$. Based on the table in Appendix 4C and the discussion in Appendix 4D you see that $d_l < 1.677 < 1.721$, so Test 5 is again satisfied and therefore the result for this model is indeterminate with respect to serial correlation. Our calculated DW is close to d_u and all the t-statistics are quite large. Thus, we might not be too concerned about this result. Even if there is some upward bias in the t-statistics it is not likely to be enough to change our finding that there is a statistically significant relationship between jewelry sales and the four independent variables in the model.

Step 5: Check for Multicollinearity

Again we need to consider whether or not there may be multicollinearity. To check for this we look at the bivariate correlations between all pairs of independent variables. This is shown in Table 10.9. We see that there are no correlations that would be high enough to cause multicollinearity.

Observations

By reading the process of developing and evaluating these models for A&F sales and jewelry sales you will have solidified your understanding of multiple regression analysis. You will really learn about regression best by doing regression. You can start by entering the data from Table 3.1 for annual women's clothing sales (WCS) into your own Excel file. Use the WCS data as your dependent variable and the year (time index) as your dependent variable. Then do the regression and verify that you get the same results as you saw in Chapter 3. After that, start to experiment with your own data.

What You Have Learned in Chapter 10

- You understand how to develop regression models
- You know how to apply the five step evaluation process to specific regression models.
- You understand how seasonal dummy variables can be selected so that all have positive coefficients and are statistically significant.
- You recognize how using seasonal dummy variables can sometimes greatly increase the explanatory power of a model.

CHAPTER 11

The Formal Ordinary Least Squares (OLS) Regression Model

Chapter 11 Preview

When you have completed reading this chapter you will be able to:

- Understand how software packages calculate the least squares regression estimate.
- Know the rule that every software package uses to choose the best regression estimate.
- Understand how R-square is calculated.
- Know how to use the Akaike Information Criterion (AIC) to choose independent variables correctly.
- Know how to use the Schwartz Criterion (SC) to choose independent variables correctly.

Introduction

You now have a good understanding of applied regression analysis. You can now do simple and sophisticated forms of regression. You know how to evaluate and interpret regression models. Some of you may be interested in the mathematics that forms the foundation of ordinary least squares (OLS) regression. You will get a start on this formal understanding as you read this chapter.

A Formal Approach to the OLS Model

In mathematical notation, the true simple linear regression is expressed as:

$$Y_i = \alpha + \beta X_i + \varepsilon_i$$

where

Y_i = the value of the dependent variable for the ith observation

X_i = the value of the independent variable for the ith observation

ε_i = the value of the error for the ith observation

α = intercept of the true regression line on the vertical, or Y, axis. (This may also be called the constant term in regression software.)

β = slope of the true regression line

Normally, the data do not follow an exactly linear relationship. In the scattergram in Figure 11.1, for example, it is impossible to draw one straight line that will go through all the points. The method of OLS is a way of determining an equation for a straight line that best (according to the least squares criterion) represents the relationship inherent in the data points of the scatter diagram. The general form of this estimated linear function may be stated as:

$$Y_{iE} = a_E + b_E X_i$$

where a_E and b_E are the calculated (or estimated) values of the intercept and the slope of the line, respectively. Y_{iE} is the calculated value for the dependent variable that is associated with the independent variable X_i.

Since the (Y_{iE}) values are all located on the "calculated" straight line, the actual Yi values will, in most cases, differ from your calculated (Y_{iE}) values by a residual amount, which are denoted as e_i. (These residuals may also be referred to as deviations, or errors.). Mathematically, this can be expressed as:[1]

$$Y_i - Y_{iE} = e_i$$

and thus,

$$Y_i = Y_{iE} + e_i$$

Further, since you have defined $Y_{iE} = a_E + b_E X_i$, this expression may be written as:

$$Y_i = a_E + b_E X_i + e_i$$

---

[1] The subscript E following a term refers to an estimated value.

There are at least two reasons for the existence of the residual (e_i) in the previous equation:

1. It is impossible to know and have data for all the factors that influence the behavior of the dependent variable
2. There are errors in observation and measurement of economic data.

Thus, it is normally impossible for one straight line to pass through all the points on the scatter diagram, and it becomes necessary to specify a condition that the line must satisfy to make the line in some sense better than any of the other lines that could be drawn through the scatter diagram. The OLS condition can be stated as follows:

The line must minimize the sum of the squared vertical distances between each point on the scatter diagram and the line.

In terms of Figure 11.1, the line must minimize the sum of the squared residuals, that is, minimize Σe^2.

The linear relationship, or line, that satisfies this condition is called an OLS regression line. The expression for the sum of the squared vertical distances is:

$$\Sigma e_i^2 = \Sigma (Y_i - Y_{iE})^2$$
$$\Sigma e_i^2 = \Sigma (Y_i - a_E - b_E X_i)^2$$

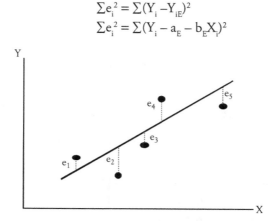

Figure 11.1 The OLS regression line for Y as a function of X. Residuals (or deviations or errors) between each point and the regression line are labeled e^i

where each expression is summed over the n observations of the data, that is, for i = 1 to i = n. In this expression, the a_E (the Y intercept) and b_E (the slope) are the unknowns, or variables. Given this equation, the objective is to obtain expressions, or normal equations, as they are called by statisticians, for a_E and b_E that will result in the minimization of $\Sigma\, e_i^2$.

The normal equations are:[2]

$$b_E = (\Sigma Y_i X_i - nY_M X_M) \div (\Sigma X_i^2 - nX_M^2)$$
$$a_E = Y_M - b_E X_M$$

where Y_M and X_M are the means of Y and X, respectively.

These two equations can then be used to estimate the slope and intercept, respectively, of the OLS regression function. Every software package that calculates OLS regression results uses these normal equations. Most of you have a calculator that does a trend and/or a bivariate regression. These normal equations are the basis for those functions in your calculator. These same normal equations are the basis of regression models estimated by every software package.

As a matter of course, you would not use these normal equations to estimate the intercept and slope terms for regression problems manually. Today, computers and appropriate software are available to everyone seriously interested in performing regression analyses. Statistical and forecasting software such as ForecastX, SAS, and SPSS, all provide good regression procedures. As you have seen, even Microsoft Excel has the capacity to calculate regression (albeit without producing some of the summary statistics needed for business use).

The Development of R-square

You learned about the coefficient of determination (R-squared) and about how it can be interpreted as the percentage of the variation (i.e., "up and down movement") in a dependent variable that can be explained by a regression model. Now that you know what R-square is, let us consider how this measure can be developed.

---

[2] The subscript M following a term refers to a mean value.

The total variation in Y is measured as the sum of the squared deviations of each Y value from the mean value of Y.

Figure 11.2 will help you to see why this summary statistic is used to measure the variation in Y. The large dot represents a single observation on two variables, X and Y. In Figure 11.2, you can see the following:

- **Total variation** = distance between the data point (Y_i) and the reference line at the mean of $Y(\overline{Y})$.
- **Explained variation** = distance between the reference line at the mean of $Y(\overline{Y})$ and the regression estimate $(\hat{Y})$
- **Unexplained variation** = distance between the data point (Y_i) and the regression line $(\hat{Y})$.

In Figure 11.2, the horizontal line drawn at the mean value for Y (i.e., Y_M) is called the reference line. The single data point shown is not on the regression estimated regression line. The amount by which the

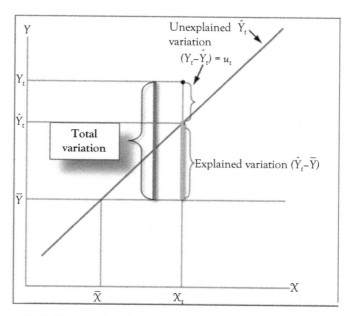

Figure 11.2 Partitioning the variation in Y. The total variation in the dependent variable (Y) can be separated into two components: Variation that is explained by the regression model and variation that is unexplained

observation differs from the mean of Y is shown by the distance labeled "total variation."

Part of that total variation in Y is explained by the regression model, but part is unexplained. Let's look at the latter. The difference between each observed value of Y and the value of Y determined by the regression equation is a residual variation that has not been explained or accounted for (see the segment labeled "unexplained variation").

The part of the total variation in Y that is explained by the regression model is called the "explained variation." For each observation, the explained variation can be represented by the distance between the value estimated by the regression line ($\hat{Y}$) and the mean of Y ($\bar{Y}$).

Does it not make sense that the sum of the "explained" plus the "unexplained" variations should equal the total variation? Note that the distance labeled "total variation" in Figure 11.2 is the sum of the "explained" and "unexplained" variations. This makes it possible to measure the total variation in Y and explain how much of that variation is accounted for by the estimated regression model.

This brings us back to the coefficient of determination (R^2). Recall that R-square is the percentage of the total variation in Y that is explained by the regression equation. Thus, R-square must be the ratio of the explained variation in Y to the total variation in Y:

$$R^2 = (\text{Explained variation in } Y) \div (\text{Total variation in } Y)$$

The Akaike and Schwarz Criteria[3]

Sometimes the diagnostic tools you have looked at thus far can be contradictory in helping us identify the "best" regression model from among some set of alternatives. This is particularly likely when the various models have different numbers of independent variables. Thus, you sometimes want to consider two other measures that can be helpful in selecting a model.

---

[3] Both of these measures, may be reported in the regression output you obtain from some software. They are not available from Excel. For a description of the mathematics behind both the AIC and the SC see: George G Judge, et al. *Introduction to the Theory and Practice of Econometrics*, 2nd ed. (New York: John Wiley & Sons, 1988), chapter 20.

One such measure calculated in many commercially available software programs is the Akaike information criterion (AIC), which considers both the accuracy of the model and the principle of parsimony (i.e., the concept that fewer independent variables should be preferred to more, other things being equal). The calculation of AIC is mathematically complex but what is important here is to know that it is designed such that lower absolute values are preferred to higher ones. In AIC, as additional independent variables are included in the model the value of AIC will increase unless there is also sufficient new information to increase accuracy enough to offset the penalty for adding new variables. If the absolute value of AIC declines significantly, after adding a new independent variable to the model, accuracy has increased enough after adjustment for the principle of parsimony.

The Schwarz criterion (SC) is quite similar to AIC in its use and interpretation. However, it is very different in its calculation, using Bayesian arguments about the prior probability of the true model to suggest the correct new model. A significantly lower absolute value for SC is preferred to a higher one, just as with AIC. If the absolute value of SC decreases after the addition of a new independent variable, the resulting model is considered superior to the previous one.

Building and Evaluating Three Alternative Models of Miller's Foods' Market Share

In this section, you will work through the process of building regression models for the Miller's Foods' market share data that you saw earlier in Chapter 7. You will consider three competing models. In the process you also expand on your knowledge of regression modeling by using the AIC and SC criteria.

Scattergrams of Miller's Foods' Market Share with Potential Independent Variables

It is a good idea to start your regression modeling by looking at graphic representations of the relationship between the dependent variable and the causal independent variables that are being considered for the model. In this example, you are going to consider price (P), advertising (AD), and an index of competitor's advertising (CAD) as potential factors influencing Miller's market share. These scattergrams, in Figure 11.3, only tell part of the story, but they can be a useful first step in getting a feel for the relationships that are involved.

The Statistical Hypotheses

Your hypotheses about these independent variables can be summarized as:

For Price: $H_0 : \beta_1 \geq 0;$ $H_1 : \beta_1 < 0$

Rationale: As price rises, people buy less from Miller's and share falls.

For Advertising: $H_0 : \beta_2 \leq 0;$ $H_1 : \beta_1 > 0$

Rationale: When advertising increases, sales and share increase as well.

For the competitors' index of advertising:

$H_0 : \beta_1 \geq 0;$ $H_1 : \beta_1 < 0$

Rationale: As the index rises, competitors are advertising more and Miller's loses market share.

In each of the advertising scattergrams (see Figures 11.3B and 11.3C) you see visual support for the hypotheses suggested above. However, for the price scattergram (Figure 11.3A), the hypothesis seems incorrect. This is likely due to the fact that you are examining price alone without the two other variables that you know act with it to determine sales.

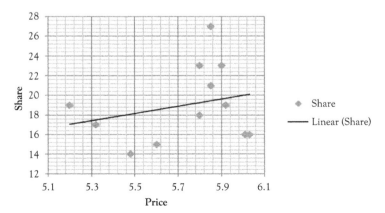

Figure 11.3A Scattergram of Miller's Foods' market share with price

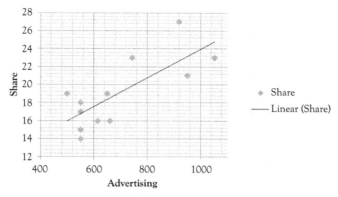

Figure 11.3B Scattergram of Miller's Foods' market share with advertising

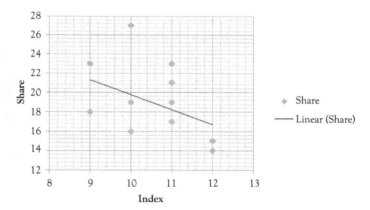

Figure 11.3C Scattergram of Miller's Foods' market share with the index of competitor's advertising

The Three Alternative Models

With three possible independent variables there are many alternative models that you could construct. Consider the following three regression models:

$$Share = f\,(Price)$$
$$Share = f\,(Price, Advertising)$$
$$Share = f\,(Price, Advertising, Index)$$

Rather than show the results for these models in the form of their respective computer printouts they are summarized in Table 11.1. When a number of alternative models are presented, it is a common practice to organize the results in a table such as this to facilitate easy comparison between them.

From the information in Table 11.1, you can perform the five-step evaluation process. First, the signs on all coefficients in all of the models are consistent with our expectations (with the exception of price in the simple regression shown in Model 1), so the models make sense from a theoretical perspective. Second, all of the t-ratios are large enough (with the exception of price in Model 1 and Model 2) to allow us to reject the corresponding null hypotheses. Thus, in general you find statistically significant relationships.

The coefficients of determination vary from a low of 6.58 percent to a high of 81.17 percent. Model 3 has an adjusted R-square of 81.17 percent which means that 81.17 percent of the variation in Miller's Foods' market share is explained by variation in price, advertising, and the index of competitors' advertising.

The DW statistic for the three models improves as variables are added. For Model 3, the DW statistic of 2.17 indicates possible negative serial correlation, but it is likely not severe enough to be of concern given

Table 11.1 Three OLS multiple regression models for Miller's Foods' market share

Variable	OLS Model 1	OLS Model 2	OLS Model 3
Intercept	−2.05	17.79	80.01
P	3.67 (0.84)	−1.87 (−0.55)	−8.46 (−3.13)
AD	−	0.02 (3.46)	0.02 (6.40)
CAD	−	−	−2.54 (−3.92)
R-square or Adjusted R-square	6.58%	51.03%	81.17%
Durbin–Watson	0.63	1.39	2.17
Std. Error of Est.	3.91	2.70	1.68
SC	66.62	56.46	43.58
AIC	67.10	56.94	44.06

*Values in parentheses are t-ratios.

how large the t-ratios are in Model 3. The DW of 2.17 satisfies Test 2 in Appendix 4D indicating the result is indeterminate. If the calculated DW statistic was between 2 and 2.072, Test 3 would be satisfied indicating no serial correlation.

Finally, you should check the correlation matrix to evaluate the potential of multicollinearity. The correlation matrix for the independent variables is:

	P	AD	CAD
P	1.00		
AD	0.47	1.00	
CAD	−0.59	−0.09	1.00

None of these correlations among the independent variables indicates the presence of severe multicollinearity.

Note that as each variable is added to the simple regression, the AIC and SC decrease by 10 or more points; this indicates that each variable added is likely to be a correct variable to include in the model.

What You Have Learned in Chapter 11

- You understand how software packages calculate the least squares regression estimate.
- You know the rule that every software package uses to choose the best regression estimate.
- You understand how R2 is calculated.
- You know how to use the AIC and the SC to evaluate regression models correctly.

APPENDIX

Some Statistical Background

You often use statistics to describe data. In doing so, measures of central tendency and measures of dispersion are often used. In this appendix you will have a chance to review these concepts. Doing so may help you better understand some aspects of regression analysis.

Population versus Sample

Before discussing some descriptive statistics let us take a little detour to talk about populations and samples. A population represents the entire list of all possible measurement units. Some examples might help you understand this. Suppose you are interested in developing a model for sales at individual Abercrombie & Fitch stores in 2016. The population would be all Abercrombie & Fitch stores that were in business in 2016. If you were doing a study concerning students at the University of Iowa, the population would be all 31,387 students.

A sample is a subset of the population. Usually it is either impossible or very costly (or both) to use an entire population in a study. Think about trying to do a study that involves the entire population of students at the University of Iowa. It would be very difficult to locate and get the cooperation of all 31,387 students. And, even if you were successful, there are often students who drop out or enroll so the population changes frequently. To study students at the University of Iowa you would select a sample, or subset, of all students.

There are many ways in which you might select the sample. Some are good and others are not so good. A statistics text or a research methods text would provide you with information about the various ways by which you might select a sample. The important point here is for you to understand that you almost always work with only a subset of all the possible data. That is you work with a sample of data. It turns out that for various reasons a well-selected sample is likely to provide a more accurate view of the population than a census of the entire population.

The measures that you obtain from a sample are called statistics. The average height of students at the University of Iowa calculated from a sample of perhaps 400 students would be a statistic. The actual average height for all University of Iowa students is some value that is unknown and maybe unknowable. This value is called a population parameter. You can get a good estimate of the true height of all University of Iowa students by using the average height based on your sample of 400 students (assuming you did a good job of selecting the sample).

In all aspects of statistical work you use **S**ample **S**tatistics to estimate **P**opulation **P**arameters. Note the S's go together and the P's go together, which makes this relationship easy to remember. In statistical work, sample statistics are normally represented by English letters and population parameters are typically represented with Greek letters. For example, a sample mean is denoted $\bar{x}$, while a population mean is denoted μ.

Central Tendency

When you want to describe to someone the general case for some measurement, you use a measure of central tendency which may represent a "typical" case in the population. There are three primary measures of central tendency: (1) the mean, (2) the median, and (3) the mode.

The Mean

The mean is often called the average. You may have seen the mean represented by the symbol $\bar{x}$. To calculate the mean you add the values of all observations on the measurement and then divide by the number of observations. Suppose you have the following five observations: 1 5 3 4 2. When added these equal 15. To get the mean you would divide this sum by the number of observations (five). So, for this simple example, you get the mean as:

$$\bar{x} = 15/5 = 3.$$

The Median

The median is another measure of central tendency. The median is the value that is in the middle of the data set if the values are arrayed from low to high (or high to low). Using the same five observations used afore, if you order them from low to high you have: 1 2 3 4 5. The middle value is 3, so that is the median. In this case, the median and the mean are equal.

Think about this: What if in the data the five was 500? What effect would this have on the mean and the median? If the 5 was changed to 500 the data set would be: 1 2 3 4 500. The mean would now be 510/5 = 102. But, what about the median? The median is still 3. When you have data with one or more values that are very high or very low compared to other values the median might better represent the "typical" case than would the mean.

When you have an even number of observations there is no middle number. Consider these data: 1 2 3 4 5 6. There is no number that splits the data into two equal halves. In such a case, you use the average of the two middle values to represent the median (3 and 4 in this example). So you would say the median is 3.5.

The Mode

The mode is the value that occurs most frequently in a set of data. Consider the following data: 1 3 4 2 5 6 2 7 2 6. The mode would be equal to 2 since that value appears three times while other values appear only once or twice.

Dispersion

There are three measures of the degree of dispersion in data that are most common. These are the range, the standard deviation, and the variance. In addition, you will see a measure of dispersion called a "standard error." This is a measure of dispersion for a statistic rather than for data.

The Range

The range for data is the distance between the lowest and the highest values. When provided in addition to a measure of central tendency, the range gives you a better feel for the data. Consider again the following data: 1 3 4 2 5 6 2 7 2 6. The range would be from 1 to 7.

The Standard Deviation

The standard deviation is a common way to express the average distance between each value and the mean of all the values. For the values 1 3 4 2 5 6 2 7 2 6 the mean is 3.8. None of the actual values equals the mean and each is some distance away from the mean.

The standard deviation is calculated by subtracting the mean from each of the 10 values and squaring that result. These values are then added together and divided by $n - 1$ (where n is the number of observations). Finally, you take the square root of that value to get the standard deviation. You normally use the letter s to represent the sample standard deviation. The population standard deviation is the Greek letter sigma (σ) and is calculated in a similar manner except that the denominator is just n and the population mean μ is used in the numerator rather than the sample mean ($\bar{x}$). The calculation is:

$$s = \text{Standard Deviation} = \sqrt{\frac{\Sigma(X - \bar{X})^2}{(n - 1)}}$$

The Variance

The variance is the square of the standard deviation. So the variance is given by:

$$s^2 = \frac{\Sigma(X - \bar{X})^2}{(n - 1)}$$

You may wonder why both are important when one is just the square of the other. The standard deviation is much more easily understood by people as a measure of dispersion than is the variance. However, the variance has some very nice statistical properties that can be useful in advanced forms of data analysis. In fact, you could take a full semester course just studying analysis of variance (ANOVA) ... that is, studying various aspects and applications of the simple formula: $= \dfrac{\Sigma(X - \bar{X})^2}{(n - 1)}$

To help you understand this, consider a hypothetical situation. Suppose you own a car dealership that sells an average of 364 cars a month. When you are reading a newsletter from a car dealer association you read that nationally the mean car sales per month for dealers is 400. That piece of information you would understand and could relate to your business.

As you read further you see that the variance is given as 10,000 cars squared per month. Wow!! That would be confusing. The 10,000 is a really big number in your mind and you are really confused by what a "car squared" means. You know what a Ford Focus is. But what is a Ford Focus squared? You see that a variance is not such a good way to describe dispersion to someone. But, what if you find the square root of 10,000 cars squared? It would be 100 cars and is the standard deviation. This is something that would make sense to you.

The Standard Error

It is easy for you to see that there is dispersion in data. But what about statistics? Is there a measure of dispersion for statistics? The answer is yes. Suppose that you and five friends do an experiment in which each of you go to a mall and randomly select seven people to interview. Each of you ask each person in your sample of seven some questions, one of which might be their ages. All six of you have a sample of seven ages. Do you think all six of the average ages from your six samples would be exactly the same? It is very (very very) unlikely. What is likely is that all six average ages will be different. They might be 34.5, 23.8, 46.7, 50.3, 23.9, and 32.7. You see that there would be a range from 23.8 to 50.3. That is, there would be dispersion in the sample statistic ($\bar{x}$).

A standard error is a measure of dispersion for a sample statistic and is analogous to a standard deviation. You will see the term standard error a number of times in the text and when you do regression in Excel. So now you have some idea what this term means.

Index

OTHER TITLES IN QUANTITATIVE APPROACHES TO DECISION MAKING COLLECTION
Donald N. Stengel, California State University, Fresno, Editor

- *Service Mining: Framework and Application* by Wei-Lun Chang
- *Regression Analysis: Unified Concepts, Practical Applications, and Computer Implementation* by Bruce L. Bowerman, Richard T. O'Connell, and Emily S. Murphree
- *Experimental Design: Unified Concepts, Practical Applications, and Computer Implementation* by Bruce L. Bowerman, Richard T. O'Connell, and Emily S. Murphree
- *An Introduction to Survey Research* by Ernest L. Cowles and Edward Nelson
- *Business Applications of Multiple Regression, Second Edition* by Ronny Richardson
- *Business Decision-Making: Streamlining the Process for More Effective Results* by Milan Frankl
- *Operations Methods: Managing Waiting Line Applications, Second Edition* by Kenneth A. Shaw

Announcing the Business Expert Press Digital Library
Concise e-books business students need for classroom and research

This book can also be purchased in an e-book collection by your library as

- a one-time purchase,
- that is owned forever,
- allows for simultaneous readers,
- has no restrictions on printing, and
- can be downloaded as PDFs from within the library community.

Our digital library collections are a great solution to beat the rising cost of textbooks. E-books can be loaded into their course management systems or onto students' e-book readers.
The **Business Expert Press** digital libraries are very affordable, with no obligation to buy in future years. For more information, please visit **www.businessexpertpress.com/librarians**. To set up a trial in the United States, please email **sales@businessexpertpress.com**.